T0147311

ONYA

written by Ann Loera

iUniverse, Inc.
New York   Bloomington

O N Y A

iUniverse books may be ordered through booksellers or by contacting:

iUniverse
1663 Liberty Drive
Bloomington, IN 47403
www.iuniverse.com
1-800-Authors (1-800-288-4677)

Because of the dynamic nature of the Internet, any Web addresses or links contained in this book may have changed since publication and may no longer be valid. The views expressed in this work are solely those of the author and do not necessarily reflect the views of the publisher, and the publisher hereby disclaims any responsibility for them.

ISBN: 978-1-4502-4541-8 (sc)
ISBN: 978-1-4502-4542-5 (ebook)

Printed in the United States of America

iUniverse rev. date: 7/28/2010

Dedicated to my dad and mom, Bill and Mary,
my husband Rene',
and our two sons Christopher and Matthew

Chapter 1

It is 2010, and I am 63 years of age. I feel I have lived three separate lives. Actually, I might not have been born in 1947. My mom and dad lived on my grandparent's farm, in a small cottage adjacent to the huge farm house. My mom was heavily pregnant with me when the cottage caught on fire. She barely managed escape by grabbing my two older sisters; and, running out as fast as she possibly could, considering her condition. Fortunately, no one was hurt, but they lost everything they owned. Which was not much in those days. Since that time, Mom doesn't even enjoy a lit candle. While still an infant, I was baptized "Onya Vasilevna". All four of my grandparents came from Russia in the first decade of 1900. My mom and dad were born in America and married Russians. Thus, I became 2nd generation Russian-American.

My childhood was totally different Oh no, not American, like you or your best friend from across the street. That was my first life. I grew up in a family of four daughters. We went to church every Sunday, and also during the Russian/Orthodox religious holidays. My mom and dad dressed in the traditional church attire, as was done in faraway Russia. My bunya (grandmother) and deda (grandfather) carried the tradition across the sea. The men's shirt had buttons up one side near the neck area, and a matching colored sash worn around their waist, similar to a Cossack shirt. The women wore a long skirt and blouse decorated with lace, buttons, and/or sequins, including a lacey head shawl (kasinka). The married couples wore the same matching color.. Only the color white for funerals, but colored matching outfits for other church events were allowed.

I even remember going to funerals, where the body was laid out in the coffin in the people's living rooms. And you think I grew up normal. Later! Nowadays, the coffins are transported from the mortuary to the Russian church.

And a lot of these houses were located on farms. So back then, they only had outhouses.

Those were located some distance from the house, normally on a well-worn dirt path. Oh, and, by the way, no outside lighting. It would have been cool to see solar lights on a nice-smooth cement walkway.

It was very dark outside, not to mention the animal sounds and smells. Was I brave enough to walk alone? No way! I would drag someone along who was just as scared as I was. We were afraid of the bogeyman.

Chapter 2

Hopefully when you read this, rice krispies with marshmallows will still be around. One relative of ours, whenever we visited, the oldest daughter automatically started preparing these delicious treats. No baking needed so they were ready to eat within minutes. Melt real butter in sauce pan, add a bowl of rice krispies and marshmallows together. Melt and form into a pan. Then simply cut into squares. Delicious! And the butter, was most likely made right there in their home, by the mother.

My family also had two cows when we lived on the farm. We named them Suzie and Anna. I remember my own mom making butter, buttermilk, and cheese. And, yummy: fresh homemade bread. Before the bread even cooled from the oven, I would slice off a chunk, and slather it with that good ol' homemade butter. Can you even guess the calories in that production?

Besides our two cows, he had numerous chickens, turkeys, and endless dogs and cats. We had 20 acres and my dad planted cotton. My dad also worked full-time at a furniture factory. The income from the land alone would not sustain a family of six, sometimes more. The Russian way, you never turned down family if they came to visit. And that often included grandparents needing a place to live. Motels were unheard of. It was just our way of life.

Chaper 3

While my dad was at work at the furniture factory, one beautiful, courageous day, my younger sister Manya and I decided we wanted to help our dad, because he was very tired from having two full-time jobs. So, we proudly chopped two rows of cotton. Mind you, now, chopping cotton does not include the cotton plants, only the weeds. Well, naturally we did not know the difference, aged about 5 and 6, and literally cut down two complete rows, cotton and all. Angry cannot best describe my dad's reaction when he arrived home, hot and tired after a full day away.

My dad had another angry time when his workers were picking cotton, and throwing the bags into a large hopper, with a plank across the middle, so they can walk on it and empty out the bags of cotton. When he was busy and not looking, my younger sister and I would climb up onto the plank, and jump into the huge mounds of soft, fresh, clean, new cotton balls. That lasted all of one or two jumps, before he saw us destroying the fresh, clean cotton.

About my two-prized cows, Anna and Suzie, I remember petting them and looking into their eyes, and exclaiming, "You have big brown eyes just like me". I enjoyed those cows. When my dad sold the farm, he sold the cows to yet another family relative, who owned a large spread, close to be calling a ranch. Unfortunately, I later heard my cows died choking on some bail wire, from the haystacks.

Next to our barn, was a hayloft, with the only access a ladder, placed near the entrance. I remember all four of us girls climbing up, me and my younger sister, dragging along our little tricycles. There was a stove and a bed in that hayloft. That was our retreat whenever we needed to escape our mom. My older sisters would pull the ladder up so my mom couldn't climb up. She was yelling up at us, to come down. Were we crazy? If we came down, the belt would be waiting . No way, Jose! One time we were up there for hours, and we were starving. My oldest sister, Tanya, made us spaghetti.

Chapter 4

I recall spending some time at my bunya and deda's farm. They had vineyards which they cultivated for raisins, not wine. They had a good amount of acreage, and deda had a small train on tracks, and wagons to transfer the fruit from the vineyards to the barnyard. Sometimes he would let me sit in one of the wagons, and away I would go.

Vineyards prepared for raisins required much work. The grape bunches were picked, laid on rolled paper along the rows, and left to dry. Once dry, the pickers would go back to the rows, and pick up the bunches of raisins. A long back-breaking process.

The Russian families only ate kosher meats. My bunya and deda also raised chickens. The women had placed tables in the shade, and there were huge pots filled with steaming, boiling water. About thirty feet away, the men were grabbing the chickens running around. I watched in fascination. Deda had a big wooden block and I stood to one side of it. One of the men would hand me a squirming and squawking chicken. I held on to it tightly around its chest area. Then my deda would approach the block on the other side, and wham-o, he cut off its head, with a butcher knife. Without delay, I needed to run away from everyone with that chicken, dripping blood and still moving. Once I ran a good distance, I threw it on the ground, and watched it jumping around until it stopped. Shortly later, this dead chicken was placed in the boiling water so it would be relatively easy to pluck. I never liked that job. First off, the water burned my hands, and secondly, plucking was difficult for me. I was under ten years old at the time.

The significance of this next encounter baffles me. Of course, it is in the 1950's. I had a play-friend on the side of the house. An old, black Ford car. It had no engine, upholstery was shot, but I would play in it for hours at a time. It was cool inside, and the weather in the summer could get into the 100's. Just my rag dolls and me. Well, one day my folks apparently hired a man to come out and disassemble the car and tow it away. I remember standing inside the house, looking out the window, and what I saw, literally changed something in my small brain. There was a huge, and I mean, huge, black man without his shirt on. He was all shining and glistening, breaking and tearing apart my toy. I remember to this day, as I sit here at age 63, that I started screaming and yelling for him to stop. I've been told by my mom, that for weeks after, I would not talk, became very quiet and introverted. I, of course do not remember any of this, because I was so traumatized. Not knowing what to do herself, my mom told her mom, my bunya, who came over and prayed for me. My mind eventually opened up again, and I became a normal child. Talking about my bunya, when I was a bit older, pre-teen, I would continuously get sty's. A large, ugly red, pimple-like growth on my eyelids. My bunya would once again say some sort-of prayer and "spit in my eye". Yes, indeed, a true spit. But you know, it healed and did go away. After pre-teen, I still got these growths, and no way, was I having my bunya "spit in my eye". I mixed a solution of one teaspoon honey with sulfur, a yellow powder, and hello there, swallow the concoction. It worked like a charm.

One day when I was about seven, I was playing outside the house. I found a can of gasoline in the yard. My dad used this for his tractor. I used to like the smell of the gasoline fumes when we stopped at the gas stations. So, guess what I did. I stuck my head inside the can and totally spaced out. I was hallucinating badly. I looked up at the telephone poles and wires. There were angels and devils arguing with each other, back-to-back. Hundreds of them standing and arguing across the telephone lines. As I started falling backwards, my dad saw me from the kitchen, and ran out and caught me before I hit my head. As if I did not already do enough damage to my head.

Chapter 5

When my folks sold the farm, we moved closer to his factory. Across from us was a grove of fig trees. There were always bees all over the place. Back then most moms did not work outside the home. During summers, the neighborhood moms would turn on the sprinklers in their front yards. We would run up and down in our swimming suits.

No one had an automatic sprinkling system. The moms just kept moving the little sprinkler from section to section. No one complained that we were running through their yards. Nowadays, I know from personal experience, if I saw any kid playing in my front yard, I would shoo him away. The yards of today are for appearance-sake only. Heaven forbid if it got all mashed down. I remember always stepping on bees. Just sat down, yanked up my foot, and wham-o, pulled out that sticker. No crying or sulking.

While I was a teenager, I was absolutely forbidden to go to church, as well as every adult woman, if we were having our monthly. Unclean, you see. And no sex Saturday night for the married. Like who in the heck is going to know if you had sex or not! Well, did I date when I was in high school? Not unless the date was a Russian boy. My parents did not allow me to date nin-nash (non-Russian). My high school had not one Russian boy attending. I had four or five real close Russian boy (friends) who I hung around with. But never too date. They even called my folks "mom and dad".

I was also not allowed to be a member of the 4-H club (farm and agriculture club), nor invite girls from school for an overnight party. So you do see why I felt an outsider. I felt very deprived. I remember saying "Mom, can I invite Mary Ann over to spend the night?" Mom would say "Newt douschka" (daughter) "Why can't I join the swimming team?" "Newt douschka". Most of the Russians lived on the outlying farms, where they raised cows and farmed produce.

I loved the fair. Most likely the only reason I was allowed to attend was because my dad also loved the fair. So, I did go, along with my Russian friends, Nick, Bill and Al. Their parents were obviously more generous with their children, giving them a little more freedom with the outside world. We would sit around on the fences where their pet cow or sheep were on display. This, by the way, was an all-day event. And us who live in the 21st century, with all our hi-tech equipment., would be texting, playing games, sending messages. We just simply sat there and talked and laughed and had so very much fun. Ahhh YOUTH!

Back then we had drive-ins, which I will get to in a minute. So, we would all pile in someone's car for the night. Like one night, Nick and I thought it would be hilarious to pretend we were a married couple. We had the windows rolled down, and Nick and I would yell at the top of our heads. "Nick you so and so." And, Nick, while driving, would pretend, to hit me. I would look out the window: "Stop it. You're hurting me". People at the stop signs would look over curiously but did nothing. Hot summer nights. What else could we do for fun?

Going to those drive-ins, some light kissing was done. Seriously here, how pathetic is it to kiss your own brother! That was about it. Too much laughing, and not enough lip-locking. So to learn French-kissing in the 60's, most young girls kissed their own wrists for practice.

Chapter 6

I matured rather largely when I was about 13 years old. I was always so self-conscious of my breasts. Forget taking showers in P.E. There was just no way I was going to disrobe and walk into a wet, cold mist, totally naked. And lord have mercy, if P.E. was my first period (now I believe they are called classes). After getting sweaty and all from whatever sport we were into. Thinking of high school, I did not have to walk, because my folks bought me a 54 Ford, yucky green color. To this day, I wish I drove it with me and kept it forever. What a classic! Instead I bought a white '63 bug when I graduated and started working.

Back to P.E., I remember first hearing about President JFK being assassinated, while standing right outside the gym. In l963, that was probably the quietist time ever recorded in the history of my school. We were high schooler's and wept openly with each other. It was announced school was closed for the rest of the day. No sense of jubilation with us kids, no way. We all left and went home to watch television.

This television set. Let me tell you something you may find unreal. It was a black and white, with antenna ears, screen 18 inches, sitting on a stand. And back then, a family of six to eight would all try to get the best view. Oh yeah, due to my being Russian and all, if we were having company over (that is guests), my mom and dad would roll the T.V. into their bedroom, to hide it. Seriously, why? Truthfully, to this day, I had been told it was our religion. "Was it because it was considered a luxury, a convenient way of communicating with the real world, a sin"? Wow, would it have been a sin in the 60's to have a T.V. when 50 years later, we have progressed so rapidly, it literally scares me. I mean, really, I grew up typing on a manual typewriter. Once I graduated, electric came in. Then in the 80's I remember hearing about Microsoft word. Holy moly, that was too cool. Imagine typing one letter and address it bulk. I mean, really, my first job, I typed contracts, 5 copies, using carbon paper. Most of you do not know what I am talking about. And if I made even one tiny error, I had to start over. No white-out or spelling check.

Whenever a cousin got married, and it was in the big city, my folks allowed us to go Greyhound to and back. Russian weddings were always on Sunday's, church services began at 10:30 am up thru 2:30 pm. During that time, the couple is wedded in Russian dialogue, too bad if you do not understand. During the wedding, there is a four-course feast. Later, the teens and "young people" all in their 20's, get together at a hall and party, called a reception. A real honest-to-goodness live band. And bar. And always, I mean, always, at midnight, the last song played, was "Goodnight my Love". Where were the newly married couple, who knows, well, on second thought, never partying with us? Then Manya and I would go homeward-bound, via Greyhound. And we were expected to go to school that Monday.

Chapter 7

I remember when we moved to a bigger house in the same city. Closer to my dad's job. I was 14 and walked to Jr. High (now ya' all call it middle school). Sometime during the day, I became quite sick and rested in the nurse's office until school was dismissed. I am a very stubborn older lady, a well as when I was a teenager. I walked home by myself. It took me forever, due to the horrible pain in my stomach. I told my mom and dad that I was ill and went to sleep early. No way did I want to interrupt my folks sleep. Besides that, hospitals and doctors cost money. I knew money was tight. So along about midnight, the pain became unbearable. I walked to the bathroom, and when I took care of business, I closed the door loudly, enough to wake my folks. My daddy came out and told me to get back in bed. He called the hospital and they told him to press on my stomach. He did, and folks, I literally doubled in half. They told him to bring me in pronto. I had emergency appendicitis surgery. Stayed in the hospital for three or four days. I was also released from P.E. for four months which was no problem to me. Yeah!!!

While I was 16-17 ½, I did have a Russian boyfriend. We wrote each other; and; one weekend, he and his friends came up North to visit. My brothers, Nick, Bill and Al moved his V.W. up onto our front lawn, while we were sleeping. They thought it was funny. My Dad thought otherwise. Yes, my boyfriend and his buddies slept in the living room. Back then, did motels exist? And, no, I never left my bedroom. We seldom saw each other, and we sort-of drifted apart when I turned 18. Then I heard he was drafted. He went to Vietnam and we started corresponding again. I graduated in 1965, without going to my prom. I did go to my graduation all-nighter. Filled a huge tub with ice, and packed it with beer. After graduation, Mary Ann and I took my mom home. My mom was the only one who attended my graduation, because my dad and younger sister moved to the big city. Anyhow, our graduation party was at some lodge or club, which included dancing, a midnight buffet, and more dancing. I so remember the song "Wolly Bully".

Mind you, I considered myself a hi-school nerd. I was often called four-eyes because I wore glasses. Since 4th grade, yet. These eyeglasses were nothing like the sleek ones of today. They were total black, and shaped like cat-eyes. Hideous. So when one popular guy invited me to dance, you betcha'. Of course, Maryann and I had been sneaking out all night to the trunk and drinking beer. Our dance movements somehow ended up in the back of the room, behind a partition. This dude started kissing and tried to fondle my breasts. I was so embarrassed and immediately fled. Think back now to my upbringing. Totally chaste. I wonder now if I was the talk of my school, having developed early and big.

During one of our trips as a family, my mom and dad cooperated with us girls, by playing a radio station we liked. One time, the song "Only the Lonely" was playing. When it finished, my mom asked if they were singing "Tony Bologna". We girls laughed so hard. It has remained in my memory forever.

Another time, we were all sitting together watching television. James Brown was singing "Please, Please, Please", while walking back and forth, on stage. Some one had placed a cape on his back. And he was kneeling and walking on his knees, on the floor, while continuing to sing. My mom said: " Hoad-ish-ka". (meaning "oh my goodness") "What is he doing"? I told her it was part of his act. She couldn't believe it. It is a good thing she no longer watches television. Our videos of today would shock her. Some of them even shock me.

Chapter 8

I had graduated in mid of June 1965 and already had a job waiting for me. In April, I took a couple of days off from school. I went to the city and applied for a position with the State as a stenographer. I was tested and interviewed on the same day. When I left to go home, I already had a hire date for the last week of June. I was very excited. I moved in with my older sister, Nadia, and started work, and enrolled in college.

When I was called into one of the offices to type a letter or contract, I actually took along my steno pad and wrote in shorthand, words that were given to me verbally. I could just see myself sitting there all prim and proper, in a business suit, writing frantically in shorthand. That is so old-school now.

A lot of our Russian families were moving to Australia to farm land. A young man I knew, from the farm days, wrote me a letter, and asked my permission to become his bride. It was naturally sent to my mom and dad's house. The most I did with that letter was to share it with my folks and decline the invitation to marry him. He was like another one of my brothers.

Chapter 9

I was no longer called "four eyes". I was fitted for hard contacts. I am not even sure if the "hard" version is still made. In the following years when my sons were in there early teens, they both wore glasses, and they were also fitted for contacts. The "soft" version, Disposables. Wear them for a month and discard. Later in life, we all three had lazar surgery. An in-office procedure where a beam is directed into the eye, and the top cornea lifted. The three surgeries were successful. No longer did I need to carry contact solution, in addition to needing night glasses to drive, in addition to wearing regular glasses at home, after I took out the contacts. Yes, it was an expensive procedure. But I definitely recommend it to anyone who qualifies for the eye surgery. I actually required two eye surgeries, because my cornea was too thin.

In 1966, during the late winter, I was invited to one of my aunt and uncle for dinner. I was almost 19 years of age, and surely that was getting too old to marry, or what? At this dinner, was another older couple with their son, six years older than me, and single. This was a set-up. A Russian set-up! Well, folks, we clicked and started dating. Somehow, and I still do not know WHY, my deda (grandfather) got involved, and a huge meeting with everyone involved, was held. This was about end of Spring. Deda asked if we loved each other, to which we said yes, and I swear, he prompted the marriage to take place as soon and possible, in case we got the "hots" for each other. And this coming from a man with 13 children, nine boys and four girls. He definitely knew what it is all about! I remember getting officially engaged around Easter time. He gave me a beautiful ring. Our wedding was set for June, so I could be a lovely June bride, every bride's dream come true.

I want all of you people in the 21st century to know I was a virgin, properly protected by mom and dad's rule, and the most I received from heavy petting was hickies. Yes, it was turning hot that time of year, and here I was wearing turtlenecks.

So June arrives and my Russian wedding dress is made, my crown, and my "kasenka"(a lacey scarf). I am dressed from top to bottom, in white, with only my face showing, and my hands and feet. Even my neck is covered with the scarf. And, hello, this is in the month of June. I married this Russian man, who I only knew for a few brief months. We actually and, I am serious here, married each other, repeating Russian words that our best man and his wife pronounced. I had no idea what I was saying. This couple who was our best man and his wife are the very same aunt and uncle who introduced us back at their house for dinner. I was a very naïve young lady. My upbringing was very restrictive. I was delighting my folks by marrying a Russian. My oldest sister, Tanya, married a "nin-nash" and my second oldest sister, Nadia, was single. I was their first child to marry a Russian man. How proud they were that day. My groom and I were ecstatic too.

After the wedding which ended around 2:30 pm, we had an appointment with the photographer. By then, the four of us were very tired. We went to our new apartment, to rest awhile before a dinner party. While I was resting, my new husband leaves for awhile. I do not know the reason. He comes back within an hour. What the heck? Where did he go? He was very evasive with an answer when he returned. We have a nice dinner celebration with the whole immediate family. Later, when we arrive home, we naturally do what all newlyweds around the world do, for centuries. I was very much in love. We feel asleep, and around 2-3am, I woke up to find I was all alone. Looky here now, this is my wedding night. I was confused and furious.

When he finally returns, I hear some sad-ass excuse about buying cigarettes. Remember, now, I am a very gullible and innocent young lady. I accept his poor-piss excuse for the time. I do not understand why. I was in-love! One morning soon after our wedded bliss, I got out of bed and stepped on his pants, which somehow found their way to my side of the bed. Marital bliss and all, ya' know. What more can I say? So, when I stepped on his pants, I felt something in his pocket. Maybe I broke whatever it was. Naturally, I looked at him real closely and he seemed to be sleeping peacefully. I picked up his pants and crept to the bathroom. What I found in his pocket aged me ten years, and made me nauseous. Ok, here in the back of my mind, I really do know something is up with him. But love conquers all. I found a syringe and paraphernalia for shooting up heroin. I placed the articles on top of the toilet. How can he deny! Of course, he told me he will stop. And good ol' me, believed him.

Chapter 10

I would like to tell you some of the encounters and scenes I went through for the next four years. First off, remember our marriage took place in June. We both continued to go to work everyday. Sometime in September, he was arrested and called me from county jail. It had to have been the first of the month, before I deposited my monthly check. You have to know where I was headed with that check. Straight to a bail bonds office. Those places are totally filthy, in mind and body. Thank goodness I now carry a small bottle of hands-cleaner in my car. I surrendered my whole check, not having any other collateral. I waited outside of the jail for hours, yes hours, when he was finally released on bail. I loved him, ya' know.

So, did he live up to his promise to quit? Give me a break here! I even went with him to some sleazy places for his connections. Me, who came from a farm town, did not even know drugs existed; sure, drank beers and smoked real cigarettes. Not marijuana. Again, I had no idea this stuff existed. A lot of times I sat in the car waiting, but then again, my safety was a big consideration, so I usually went with him. Transactions took place without my actually seeing anything.

One time he was so loaded after he injected the heroin, his druggie and I had to physically place him in the shower to sober up. Yet, I loved him.

This heroin stuff is expensive. Another time he and his druggie were out most of the night. When I awoke the next morning, lo & behold, there was a different bug parked in our carport. They had stolen a bug for parts. I do have a temper, and by this time, I demand that stolen bug be removed at once, and my bug returned.

A year or so later, the bug was totaled out in an accident. I remember having to take the bus to work, and trying to scrunch enough money for bus faire, where we kept loose change in a jar. Forget eating lunch. There was no money. So during my lunch hour, I would go to the ladies lounge and rest on one of the cots provided for women.

All four of us sisters worked at the same high-rise building in the big city. We worked on different floors and rarely saw each other. I doubt that my sisters were aware of my true circumstances. Basically I am a private person. I did not share my sob-story with anyone. I was shamed, embarrassed, and so very mixed-up due to his addiction, and alcohol usage.

So again, he gets busted, and is placed at a mountain resort facility. I get to visit him and, actually, we are allowed to kiss and hold each other. Some couples appeared to be doing much more. But what the heck, this was first-class resort time.

Another arrest led him to spend a stint of 6-9 months in jail. Not at the mountain resort this time. One fast kiss on arrival, and one fast kiss on departure. Lots of time I carpooled with his parents. It was a good two-hour drive from our homes.

Eventually upon this release, he reverted back to his heroin use and was wanted by the police for probation violation. It was late evening and he had another of his druggies over. The police knocked on the front door, went to the carport to see if we were home, went to the back door, and all this time, flashing their spotlights inside and around the apartment. Actually, it was a front duplex; we joined the landlord's. Talk about embarrassment. We all three literally crawled around on the floor, from the living room to the one bedroom, and hid in the one bathroom. If we stood up, our silhouettes would surely show. No cigarettes. All lights out. I guess this went one for an hour or so, and they finally gave up. I went to bed, only to get up early for work. I was only in my early 20's now, but probably looked like hell and aged fast. That will explain why I was able to buy drinks in bars, as coming up next.

Chapter 11

Let me get back to my first love, when I was in high school. My friend was sent to Vietnam. One Sunday, my husband and I went to a night reception. The couple married earlier that day. We danced and ordered drinks during the party. While I was walking around by myself, guess who approached me? My first boyfriend. I was shocked when he asked me, "Why did you get married?" Something then along the lines of "I thought we had something going". Oh my, what a huge mistake I made. I quickly told him it was great to see him again, and fled to find my druggie husband.

While he was in and out of jail, I started drinking by myself. Writing long love letters to him. I missed him but not his drug abuse. Was I still in-love, sure, to a point! He was my Russian husband.

Remember I mentioned his drug habit was expensive. One day he actually approached me and asked to hawk my wedding ring. After my saying a few choice words, he relented. How dare him? What is he thinking? So was our marriage still bliss? You can guess!

While he was incarcerated, I started spending time with my sister Nadia, and this led to going to nightclubs and bars. So I just started partying, and more partying. Dancing till 2 in the morning, going to someone's house for more partying (whose house, most of the time) did not know just followed the caravan. Then about 4am, the whole gang going out to breakfast. It was difficult to be faithful, but with your husband in jail, and you being intoxicated, give it up, ya' all. I chose not to tell you the truth on this matter. You can form your own opinion. We had fun, I was growing up, and, mind you, not one of these young men were Russian.

By now my wedded bliss is starting to sour. I know I married an addict. I am not that gullible, innocent young thing anymore. But guess what, he was a good Russian boy. Just what my family wanted for me. To carry on the Russian tradition for the next 70 years.

I should give him a bit of credit. He really tried to quit. For me. He drank a lot instead, and smoked marijuana. We took a trip to visit his brother and sister-in-law. To this day, I do not truthfully know what happened. Some huge fight or disagreement. He left in the bug and crashed it into a telephone pole. Broke his leg and various scratches on his body. Probably too well saturated with booze. Thank goodness another vehicle was not involved. He was arrested however, and spent a couple of days in jail before his arraignment. My sister-in-law drove me home. It was the Christmas holidays, and I called my mom and dad, and the three of us, plus my aunt and uncle, threw all my belongings into their camper shell, and loaded up my car, and I moved back home.

Chapter 12

By now, we are in year four of our separated marriage. It is 1970. I am living at home and he moved to his parent's home after release from jail. One morning while at work, I get a call from my dad and mom to tell me he was found dead, by his father, from a drug overdose. I am now 23 and he was 29. Thus, my Russian marriage ends.

The days that followed were tiresome. The funeral was arranged and his body was dressed in complete white, which is the tradition for the Russian people. White shirt with white sash, white pants and white shoes. He looked so young and innocent lying in that all-white coffin. The body is taken from the mortuary to the Russian church at 4pm. Prayers and songs are said, and guests begin to arrive. No one is actually invited. It is just a natural thing to pay your respects. After prayers at 8pm, most guests prepare to leave only to return in the morning for the burial. The immediate family, me, his folks and family, my folks and family, all remain the entire night. No rest or sleep. It will be the last time you see the deceased, after all. I remember my folks brought their camper and took turns sleeping. I lay down on the hard bench lengthwise, and tried to sleep, with my dead husband within feet of me. The church gets mighty quiet in the early morning hours. A bit spooky! Around 7-8 am, people start arriving for the day-long burial and feast. The same people who got to go home and sleep some. All of us who spent the night beside the departed, still wore the same white outfit since yesterday afternoon. More prayers and the deceased is transported to the cemetery for burial. We are given a three- hour reprieve to rest some, shower, and change into another white outfit. Always, only white - head to feet. We all return to the same church for yet more prayers, the four-course feast, and pray for his soul.

Chapter 13

I hook up with an older crowd, quite influential in city politics, who seemed to have endless money. One of the couples had a round bed. Good lord, how do you change the sheets on that "baby". My sister Nadia and I travelled a lot with this group, from 1970-1973. My sister was a bit of a hippie. That was never my style. I appreciated nice business suits for work, and short skirts to party. Wearing jeans and pants hadn't really come in yet. Too bad it did.

I am of the opinion a young women should look like a woman. Dressed sexily, with high heels, minimum makeup, but yes, some makeup. Stylish, but not trashy. You young ladies of today should start a new trend. First, let's start with wearing hats again. To match a lovely ensemble and I do not mean a print dress with a small belt, like Harriet Nelson. A sexy hat placed at an angle, could really draw men's attention.

I could almost bet on it. So get going, all ya' young things. And if heels are out of the question for the daytime, at least a 2-inch heel. Does wonders for the legs. Spiked heels, only if you can wear them without falling down, and only at nighttime. If you must wear pants or jeans, match up with a stylish shirt and short jacket with low heels. Don't forget that charming hat, placed at an angle. Try it out. Go to a train station, and see how many men look your way. You just might be surprised!

My sister and I decide to live together again, like when I graduated from hi school. We were sharing a bed in 1970 when the huge Northridge earthquake hit. That was some shaker. Soon after, we made provisions in the small house and created a separate sleeping area for her. She and I both worked. I transferred to another job closer to my home. She was working at Northrop. We were seemingly happy and content. Of course the drinking escalated. Weekends were all about partying. Endlessly! Thank goodness I only needed to drive one mile to work instead of going into downtown. Longer sleep hours.

Nadia and I are still traveling together, and vacation together. We end up in Acapulco, when Hurricane Hilda hit in 1972. She and I were riding horse back, when the clouds started coming in real dangerous-like. The horses were becoming skittish. Our guide told us by motioning his hands, and pointing to the sky, that we had to go back. Back at the hotel, we were told to take the outside steps to the various levels where our rooms were located, due to power outage. No hot meals, the restaurant in the hotel provided cold dishes, sandwiches, and plenty of booze. All curtains were closed from ceiling to floor, in case of breakage of glass windows. And we were told to sit in the middle of the lounges, away from the windows. By nightfall, the wind was blowing ferociously. We somehow staggered up to our room, something like five levels, literally hanging on tightly to the rails, which are on the outside of the hotel. An escape route obviously. But with no elevators operating, we had no choice. This was no easy task as we were quite inebriated. Again, ahhhh youth. We woke up the next morning to sunny skies, but total destruction of the entire village. Even the top roof of the hotel was floating in the ocean along with pool loungers and chairs. We had to, absolutely had to, get out of Acapulco. Back in 1972, drainage was unheard of in that party-time resort. Water was flooding the streets and obviously the airport was shut down. The hotel somehow managed to get us onboard the last bus departing from Acapulco to Mexico City. A long endless ride. End of vacation.

Chapter 14

It is still 1972-early 1973. I continue working just up the street. My sister comes in late at night from work, and we seldom connect. Then I notice a change in her.

My sister seems to isolate herself more and more. Whenever she comes out of her room, she is always drunk and obviously, from the looks of her, she is not taking care of personal hygiene. She has beautiful, gorgeous long brown hair. Kind-of a chestnut color. She looks a mess. Her hair looks like a birds nest. I am now thinking, she must have taken a leave of absence from work.

One day I was in the kitchen and she comes in, very out-of-it. Is she on drugs too? God, I pray not. I beg, literally, beg her to tell me what is wrong. She says she cannot, "They might hear her". So we are standing by the kitchen cabinet, no pantries in that era. I remember this so clearly, just like yesterday. And I ask: "who, Nadia, please tell me, who "they" are?" She is acting terrified. She keeps looking around for "them". She then whispers to me, the …………. I am totally blindsided by that. Is she in some sort of trouble at work? She does work for the government? Is someone following her? Again, she is beyond reasoning.

Let me tell you something I learned when I was in my 50's. My younger sister told me that Nadia would go to her house, but she would be hiding in the bushes outside in the front yard. She was totally paranoid. Or was she? My mom told me, one time, when we were at emergency for one of my dad's strokes, when he was in his early 90's, the following:

She told me that when Nadia would come to visit them, she was acting strange and skittish, and told them that someone was following her, and that they were bumping into her MG. I will never know the truth of this next discussion, because my mom now has dementia and she only talks about her days in Mexico, when she was a girl. She actually told me that they received a letter from someone, discussing my sister and her actions and what I assume was harassment. I begged my mom to tell me "where is that letter?" Later on reading this, you will understand my urgency. Of course, she did not know the contents or the whereabouts. I searched my dad's room and their small lockbox. No letter. I asked my mom again for more information. Understand here, my mom is my "sweet" mama, but she never received an education. So she is just re-telling what my dad read to her from the contents of this mysterious letter. My dad was in no condition to question. When he got better, I did ask him about this car bumping and letter. He told me there was no such letter. Now why would my mom tell me this? Let's get back to my sister.

Chapter 15

Soon after, she tells me she rented in apartment at the Beach. What can I do? Prevent her? Lock her up in her room? It is late September by now. I am arranging to fly to Chicago to visit my oldest sister Tanya and her family. I call Nadia and again beg her to go with me. Get away for a few days. I feel that it is necessary for her to come with me. I sense something bad. It is just a gut feeling. I call from the airport one last time, hoping to change her mind. But get no answer. I cry while boarding. I fear leaving her behind. I arrive in Chicago, and the next day, my dad calls to tell us my sister is dead.

My mom and dad have not heard from her for several days. So, they took a drive to the Beach and found her bicycle and little MG in the carport. Strange, where is she? They again go knock loudly on her door. Still no answer. My folks become concerned. At this point, my dad goes and located the manager, who uses a key to open the door. Upon opening the door, he notes the death smell, and immediately calls the police. Lord, I feel sorry for my folks! The police politely told my folks to wait outside. I cannot begin to imagine. I cry as I write this. So you can know my sister was beautiful. She had her associates and masters in engineering. One smart cookie. The police tell my folks, that it appears a self-inflicted gun wound to the head. The door was locked from the inside and no apparent forced entry or vandalism.

I suppose the police cleaned up the apartment as best as they were willing. I remember my oldest sister Tanya and I, along with her husband, went to the apartment for her belongings. There was still blood splattered on the floor and walls of the bathroom, where she died. I took on the duty of cleaning up. I remember looking for a bucket and old rags. This is the blood of my precious sister I was cleaning up. The clean water in the bucket continued to turn from pink to a nasty red and I would dump it in the tub. To this day, if you asked me, how I was able to tolerate it, I truthfully cannot answer.

So, another Russian funeral. She was dressed completely in white. Unfortunately, it was open-casket, according to the Russian religion. She was found dead a couple days after the horrific event, and her body was quite bloated. I knew she was my sister, but then again, she was so unrecognizable.

Traditionally, immediate family go to the mortuary to approve of her hair style and clothing. When her body was removed from a table on which she was placed, and picked up and put in her forever-after home, her white coffin, I saw a blood stain on the sheet, where her head was resting. I rushed to cover the spot so my folks could not see. To this day, I never heard otherwise.

During one of the prayers, it was requested by a prophet (elderly man) for my mom to place a white band around my sister's upper body. This signified that she became the bride of Christ. The next day, after the burial, was the four-course feast in church. During another prayer, while my mom and dad were standing near the preacher, it was told through one of the prophets (who received a vision) that my sister was standing right there with them. She was happy and at peace. Spooky, I know.

Chapter 16

So, back to today, 37 years later, that my sister was found dead. I am in denial about the cause of her death. My lovely sister would never do away with herself. She was too brilliant. Too beautiful. Too intelligent. Too generous. The only one of us sister's to obtain a Master's degree. Sure, it was a gun wound, yes the police searched for any entry besides the locked front door. Did my sister know some secret information and was she murdered? They found one single wine glass on her coffee table, and it was confirmed absolutely no way anyone entered and shot her, and left her apartment. My denial forces me to think differently. I want to believe she would never end her life. I loved her immensely and, to this day, I dream about her, and it is always fantastic dreams. Sometimes in my dreams I know she is dead, but at the time, I refuse to acknowledge it. This puzzle will be completed when

I die. I will see her again. Whether or not we discuss her death, we will once again be together.

It is still l973, I am still partying. After all, I am only 25-26 years of age. No actual boyfriends. Just lots of fun. Had a selection of girlfriends, whoever was available, and we would make plans to connect at our favorite place. I was living alone and sometimes the group would all come after the 2 am call, to continue partying. Earlier, I let you know my sister died in September. It is now the long Thanksgiving weekend. Julie and I go to our favorite night spot. We drink cocktails and dance. The place was packed and all the tables were occupied.. We sat at the bar stools while resting between dances. And, oh so much fun, to dance to a real live band, not a DJ. Remember now, I am young but prior to this next moment in my life, always hung around a much older crowd.

Chapter 17

A young, damn good-looking guy asks me to dance. So we dance and enjoy each other's company. Actually my being 26, I thought he was too young for me, in looks and age. He was 24. The night ends. We say good night at the nightclub but do exchange phone numbers. He calls me repeatedly for the next few weeks. We would talk, but I did not encourage him to come over. After all, he was a "baby". Eventually, he invited me to lunch, and picked me up at my work. I liked this guy. Next, he invited me to see a concert. Double-dated with his best friend. From this point on, we started dating and enjoying one another. The relationship continued to mature and eventually he started spending the nights. He was just out of a serious relationship. He brought over a few extra clothes. He met my older sister and brother-in-law. We had some good times, and he would make breakfast for all of us on Sunday mornings. He and I became an item, besides good friends. From then on, we were actually living together. He is probably one the most funniest man, to this day, that I ever met. He would make facial expressions and tell comical stories, and sometimes, I would laugh until I peed, or almost.

Our place became a kind-of stop-off for his friends. All of his friends questioned our relationship. They were telling him I was too old for him. Just not his type. After all, this guy is one good-looking "babe", and could get anyone he wants. Some cute chick who wore a size six or less. Here I was a size 14. No kidding? I am a big-boned Russian girl. I had natural brown hair, had tried, black, red, and then stayed with blonde for years. You already know that I did wear glasses since 4th grade, but at 19, I started wearing contacts. And, lord, those babies were mighty small when I removed them at night, mind you, after a night of total partying. That reminds me of one time while dancing at a different night club, still with my friend Julie, when lo & behold, one contact popped out, right there on the dance floor, with dozens of feet on the floor. Naturally, I asked the band to stop playing "pronto", and I got on my hands and knees, and searched. Guess what? I found that stupid contact. Hurray, everyone understood, and the band started up again. Crazy times.

So, this young man that I met in the fall of 1973, is Rene'. The very same one that I tried to discourage from dating. We are still together 37 years later. His friends did get to know me, and I love them like "brothers".

Chapter 18

Early in 1974, I got another job transfer. Only this time, it was like 50 miles away. I commuted to and from for years, until 1979. A lot of times a quick stop at Der Weinerschnitzle. Yes, there was a "der" in front. At some time over the years, it was removed to only Weinerschnitzle. I would pop a couple of hot dogs in my mouth while driving, and that was my lunch. At 49c each, it was a bargain.

I was still driving that long distance, was assigned various shifts including the infamous graveyard shift. It is l976, and we receive a call from my brother-in-law and niece in the early morning hours. My oldest sister is in a bad way. Apparent overdose of prescription pills and endless booze. She is at the hospital and being taken care of. I, therefore, continue on to work. As soon as I get there, Rene' calls me and tells me to come back home. I ask my sister's condition. He refuses to tell me. I tell him I am not leaving work unless he gives me specifics. Well, he gave me specifics. My oldest sister Tanya died. I left work and drove the freeway, crying the entire time.

So, on to funeral #3. This funeral is not to be performed in the Russian church. Because my sister was married to a nin-nash (non-Russian). A bad scene when she first married him. I mean, one of my eight uncles on my mom's side, actually told my folks it was their fault. They received a lot of static from the entire Russian population. Look now, it is only the 1960's, and you basically committed a tragedy within that one family by marrying outside the church. I remember my mom and dad acting quite strangely about my oldest sister. I would overhear them talking, and got the gist that she was marrying. I snoopily went into their bedroom, opened the 4th drawer of their dresser chest. That is where my dad kept all his important papers. I found a mailed, wedding announcement from my sister. I even bravely showed it to my dad and asked if we were going to her wedding. The "no" was emphatic, I clearly got the message. She should have married a nice Russian boy. (Yeah, after all, look what happened to me). Even though her marriage took place before mine.

Chapter 19

Every morning my dad would fry his one egg and melted cheese sandwich, for his lunch break. The exact same thing day-in and day-out. Plus an apple or orange; and something sweet if it was around. He wore a blue uniform to his factory. Daddy left early in the morning, so I seldom saw him unless it was school time. This must have been summertime, since I was still in bed and did not see him leave. He was like clockwork. He came home at 5 pm every evening. We had an attached garage in a tract home neighborhood. He walked into the kitchen and greeted my mom. I knew he came home because I heard the garage door close. But let me tell you, this man in the kitchen talking to my mom was no one I knew. This man was beardless. Just who in the hell was he? "Surely not my daddy". Yet upon closer examination, he was wearing the blue uniform of his trade. I looked at this stranger again, and burst into tears. It was my daddy without his long beard. He purposely shaved his beard, which is against the bylaws of the Russian people, because he felt shamed of what my oldest sister did, by marrying out. Truly, totally unheard of in those times.

So back to my oldest sister's funeral. She was buried at Rose Hills. Her husband and I went to pick out a coffin. No white coffin this time. And no white clothing. She looked lovely. In a beautiful dress that her family chose for her burial. The congregation of well-wishers were full of "nin-nash" and our Russian people. The Russians sung songs in Russian and; to, those who received the "holy spirit" from our Lord, lifted their arms and sort-of jumped up and down, or swayed from side to side, still with their arms lifted to our Lord.

Chapter 20

In 1990 my Dad was diagnosed with melanoma, a cancer of the blood. The doctor told him he could live years, or he could go as fast as four years. He was only 75 yrs of age. He did live till 91 years of age, bless my Daddy.

Time passes. Rene' and I were house hunting for months. Many of the cities where we previewed homes, were actually cow dairy farms. That early morning smell, with the heavy mist still in the air, was a definite no-no.

We found a marvelous 4 bedroom, 2- bath, with a formal dining room. After all, in 1976, we got rid of the wraparound bar, and bought a formal dining room set, complete with hutch. So our new house absolutely must have a formal dining area for formal furniture. I so wished my oldest sister was still alive to see the transformation in my house. I was proud of that dining set.

Since we bought a house together, we decided to get married. We loved each other, been living together already for six years. Besides, career-minded or not, I was 32 years old and wanted babies. So off we head to Las Vegas with our very dearest friends, as our chaperones. We were married on Nov. 10 and had a marvelous weekend. Rene's mom told him that was also their anniversary. We did not know, beforehand, that we would be celebrating the same date. Karma! The four of us did celebrate a couple years together.

But Rene didn't have the best honest, open relationship with his dad. They continuously butted heads. I have to be fair here and tell you that it was not Rene's fault. His dad was a genuine self-centered man.

Chapter 21

Rudi (with an "i") was a studio musician. He played a trumpet and most-definitely dressed the part. Sometimes he would take along my husband to rehearsal practice.

My husband was around four years old. One time, Anthony Quinn was sitting in on the rehearsal practice. My husband got to sit on his lap. One of the bonuses in show business. Rudi (with an "i") played in Las Vegas, with various studios. He even played in Elvis' movie (Fun in Acapulco) and played at Elvis and Priscella's wedding. And, if Elvis-itis is still around 20-30s years from now, I want ya' all to know that Rudi (with an "i") was presented with a gift from Elvis. A spanking brand-new Porsche! Elvis just went out and had one delivered to Rudi (with an "i") for the friendship they developed. Seriously!

Elvis and his whole group were invited to come over for a home-cooked Mexican dinner, but Elvis' manager drew the line there. Security and all, you understand. We have a bunch of old photos with Rudi (with an "i") with different singers, musicians, and movie stars. We even had an original photo from Elvis' wedding, and during one of our home parties, we showed it around. Sorry to say, it disappeared. To this day, we do not know who snatched that genuine photo. Probably worth mega bucks now.

Chapter 22

Back to my marriage. I continued to not get pregnant. Back in those days, I did not go to a doctor, nor did Rene'. By now I am 33. It was 1982, Valentine's day. My mom and dad came over. We openly discussed the problem. My dad had both of us knell in the living room, and he placed the Bible over our heads. He then said a prayer in Russian. I accepted this by nature. My husband also accepted this, since he knew about the Russian religion.

By the way, when I married him (a nin-nash), I was forever and ever turned away from being accepted in the Russian church. That's what I got for marrying someone not Russian. Well, hello here, look what I got for marrying a good, ol', nice Russian boy.

I am only allowed to attend their Russian church, for funerals and weddings, but not to partake in the actual prayers. To this day, I still feel conspicuous. The people do stare, and they do talk. The women with their hands near their mouth, and yapping away about lit' ol.' Me. Or big-o-me. Let's be honest here.

Okay, so my papa said a prayer in February. In early May, the whole family, including my sister Manya and her husband, aunts and uncles, went to Fountain of Youth, to enjoy the weekend. Rene and I slept in back of my uncle's camper. Yes, we did have sex. After all, we were married.

In early June, we borrowed my folk's camper. We vacationed at a couple of lakes and then ended back at Fountain of Youth. I remember at one stop, it was evening, and Rene' went to the pool. I later walked over to the pool, and he was swimming alone, wait a minute now, he wasn't alone! There must have been hundreds of frogs in there, leaping and splashing with him. He invited me in. No way was I going to frolic with those slimy frogs. Yes, if you are wondering, he just continued to swim with his playmates

Mind you, here, it is June and hot. I remember not feeling well, went into the laundry room, shut the door, and fell asleep on the floor. It was cool inside and I slept comfortably for a couple hours. I was still drinking and smoking, but that time, just the thought of some wine, made by stomach turn inside-out.

I declined the wine that weekend, and even smoked less. I stared suspecting I might, hopefully, be pregnant.

Probably, happened in the back of my uncle's camper shell. On June 15, I bought a pregnancy kit. Back then, you peed on a stick and waited for it to turn a certain color. If it turned blue (or whatever color that was specified in that kit), Yes for positive and No for negative. Well, guess what folks, my test proved to be positive. I threw my pack of cigarettes down the toilet. I have not had an alcoholic drink, and, to this day, I never, ever, picked up those two nasty habits. I know God intervened and gave me the gift of my babies. Why would I question that, and destroy my relationship with Jesus.

Chapter 23

Remember earlier on, I mentioned a new job which took me 50 minutes to drive to and from home. Well, it was a promotion. I was working in a parole office for a number of years, and when the two female parole agents were not in the office, I would take the female parolee to the restroom, and give her a bottle to pee in. A drug test. If she handed it back warm, I knew she actually peed in it. Occasionally I went with the parole agents to their parolees homes to interview the parolee. Are you still working, not using, checking their arms for injections, still living at place on record? That sort of questioning.

It was l969 or so, before my first husband died. The phone rang, and who do you think it was. I looked directly outside, where a gas station sat on the corner, and also a phone booth. He waved to me and we talked briefly. We were separated at the time. And, furthermore, his parole officer was in that very same office. Crazy huh? I told him to "get lost".

Well, here I was a receptionist/stenographer, and since I was doing some parole work, I decided to take the State Correctional Officer's exam. I passed and went for an interview with the State Prison Captain. So, this was my promotion. I was assigned to a minimum security prison, men's unit. Back in the 70's, only men officers worked with the male inmates. So the transition was very difficult for me. After all, the staff resented my intrusion, as well as some male inmates. I was only the third female supervising male inmates at that prison. I literally performed all the same duties, except Receiving and Release, where the inmates were disrobed, examined and showered. Mind you, when my assignment was a dorm, where the male inmates lived, my duties included walking up and down the dorm, also the toilet and shower area. The guys would jokingly invite me in, but I got along with most of them.

One time I was assigned to the Visiting Room. One of my worker inmates did something questionable, and I fired him, and wrote up a disciplinary action. Sixty days were added to his prison sentence. A few days later, while I was in the back of the visiting room, he approached me. He was super-pissed and started to get in my face. What saved me from being assaulted, were other inmates. They shoved him away from me and, said "look dude, you'll just get more time". He angrily walked away. I did thank those male inmates from a confrontation.

Chapter 24

So I am pregnant, working in the State Prison. My uniform consisted of green pants, khaki shirt with the patches sewn on the sleeves, and black shoes. I informed my sergeant and lieutenant of my delicate situation. They left my assignment in the Visiting Room, since that is the best logical place to be in case of a riot in the facility. Naturally, I would be the very first female Correctional Officer to become pregnant. So, obviously the uniform shops did not carry maternity smocks. I bought some green material, which closely matched the pants. I had a tailor make new pants and a smock. Thus, became my uniform of the day. I wore the smock over my khaki shirt, the shirt obviously not tucked into my pants.

As time went on it became noticeably risky for me to work directly with the inmate population. The captain assigned me to the Locksmith. I could not be in a safer location, as the entry to the Locksmith building was tightly protected with barbed wire and high fencing. The Locksmith taught me how to open up locks and remove the tumblers. I separated them according to color. It was a filthy job. My hands turned black immediately from the old, dirty locks. Looking back, I should have requested gloves. It passed the time. Nothing spectacular. But I did learn a new trade.

Chapter 25

My "deda", my mom's dad, was 92 years old, and he suffered a stroke, and died. It was December 1982. I went to his funeral and was obviously very pregnant, expecting the following month. I would like you all to know that my baby would have been deda's 106th grand and great-grand child. Good lord! But, remember now, my bunya and deda did have 13 children. And most of my aunts and uncles had large families.

My first baby was due around January 29th of l983. I took maternity leave earlier than with my second pregnancy. His due date passed. I knew he was a boy, because I had an amniocentesis performed. We were able to prepare for our boy baby. We played with names. Abraham was one, but we wanted to name him something from the Bible. So, Christopher finally appeared in the world on February 18th. I went for a doctor appointment the day before, and they kept me, and induced labor and delivery. It was a very long labor. I did not go to earlier breathing classes either. But those nurses told me real quickly how to breathe during labor. They had Chris' head hooked up with stress equipment. They told me he appeared stressed and the cord could be wrapped around his neck. We both continued to be monitored. Normal delivery was being questioned. Caesarian was being discussed. Along about 5 pm, baby Chris dropped and was ready to make his presence known. Pain, oh yeah. I was not given any meds at all. A fully normal vaginal birth.

Daddy Rene' was not allowed in delivery because of our lack of attendance of pre-birth classes. Baby Chris was checked, swathed in wraps, and given to me. Total completeness can only be described what I felt, and of course, total Joy! Chris was born at 5:15 pm, and weighed 6 lb 9 ozs. They allowed Christopher to sleep in a bassinet in my hospital room. Every time I looked at him, I saw a little Rene'. He looked exactly like his daddy. I go, "well what is this all about, I carried him for nine months and not a trace of myself in him?" I walked with him that evening because I was not medicated earlier. I was in heaven. My baby boy, so precious.

Christopher was a little jaundiced and the doctor told me he would need to remain at the hospital for a couple days, when I was released. That was unacceptable. No way was I leaving him there and me going home without him. Ok, so by the time I was released, Chris did go home with me, but we kept him from direct lighting for a few days. The only other significant condition Chris had when he was born, was skin dryness. Remember now, he was like 3 weeks overdue. To this day, Chris' hands are very dry and red. They actually look painful. But he uses lots of motorizing lotion.

I breast-fed my baby. And he grew steadily. He was always happy, smiling and loved people. When he was 3 months old, I returned to the prison. Put back on that uniform minus the smock. I continued to breast-feed Chris. I took along a breast pump, a little ice chest, and plenty of ice. I took this into a bathroom and pumped the milk. It stayed on ice and was good for the next day, when Chris stayed at his babysitter's. One day while at work, I walked into the Administration building, delivering paperwork. It must have been May. Gets hot that time of year. I leaked through the shirt. On khaki it shows terribly. One of the typists told me, and I immediately left and went to the truck I was driving. I had a green sweater that matched the pants. Well, you know I wore it the rest of the day, heat and all.

Chapter 27

It was July 4th. Chris was a 4 ½ months old. After that disaster of leaking milk, I started weaning Chris on baby formula. He took to it like a champ. He was a marvelous baby, happy, was growing fantastically, and slept long hours in the middle of the night. We were very blessed and fortunate. He seldom cried long spells.

So on July 4th, a little loving took place. I knew immediately that I conceived and I knew, without a doubt, it was another boy. Sure enough, I took the pregnancy test, and ya' betcha, positive. I loved being pregnant again. I could eat and eat and yes, I did gain enormous weight. Up to 222 the day my Matthew was born.

I went to the prison everyday, and had promoted to Correctional Sergeant. I started enquiring about a lateral transfer to the Records Office. Same pay, great hours, 8 to 5, and if a riot started, those gates were open for me to leave at the end of the day. I would no longer be "peace officer" status. So, I changed positions to a normal day job, as normal as possible, working behind barbed wires and double fencing.

I started showing earlier with this pregnancy, immense weight gain, and did not really lose the weight I gained with my first pregnancy. I just know the girls in the office were talking about me. About how fat I was getting. Of course, no one suspected I was pregnant again. So one day I naturally announced my pregnancy. Sure enough, some of the closer girls told me exactly what they had been thinking.

With our second baby, we considered Michael for awhile, then we changed it to Steven.

But we really wanted a Christian name. We decided on Matthew. We loved the name and thus, our Matthew arrived on March 31, 1984.

He was due a few days earlier too. It was March 26. I was hugely pregnant the end of March. We purchased a travel trailer that month and it was ready to pick up March 26. So off the three and ½ of us go to pick up our brand new trailer. It cost like $12000 and we paid in full, from a cash payoff we received from a prior house we owned. Their second lien became a balloon payment due and payable in five years.

Before we left with our brand new travel trailer, the establishment requested a couple hundred dollars more. For the hitch or whatever. I was very stubborn. So I used my pregnancy and whacked hormone issues as an avenue to refuse to pay. I started crying and complaining that my baby is due today. It worked! They got rid of us fast and probably said good riddance to the few hundred dollars.

So with Matthew's labor, it started like 48 hours before. Really! I had extremely bad lower back pressure and pain. This went on all day and night. By the 2nd morning, I called my mom and dad to come and get Christopher. I was in labor; and, they promised earlier, that they would take care of Christopher. Naturally I sobbed when they came and got Chris. My mom told me to "hush". "You're having another baby". This was around 11 am. I went back to bed and around 3 pm, the pain was getting more intense. Rene' called off work that day. I do not remember which shift he worked at the time. His job rotated the working shifts every three months. So off we head to the hospital. I was prepared for the labor room, and stayed there for hours. At 8:06 pm, my second baby boy was born. He was not stressed in the birth canal. He weighed 6 lbs 12 ozs, three more ounces than his older brother. They were 13 ½ months apart. Like having twins.

Back to the delivery room, Matthew was checked over, and given to me. He was so very precious. Cute lit' nose. I adored him. He looked like his big brother too. Right after delivery, the new mama must also deliver the birth sac. For some unknown reason, the afterbirth had attached itself to my walls, and it was not delivering naturally. The nurse took Matthew from me. There were two doctors who were literally standing there with their hands up my uterus, ripping the afterbirth out. I was in agony and screaming. I was immediately given a pain shot. The feat was accomplished. The only problem was that I slept for hours due to the injection. I did not get to enjoy my baby till the next morning. It was April lst. Matthew was given to me after his circumcision. Poor baby. I was also put under that same morning, to have my tubes tied. Eventually, Matthew and I were united. And, Matthew was also breast-fed. There is absolutely no contentment that I can name, as sitting down with your newborn at your breast. A bonding of mother and baby is so special and unique. I will always treasure those memories.

Chapter 28

You know, to this day, almost 30 years later, my husband still questions my decision to have my tubes tied. We did discuss this beforehand. I want you all to know it was a mutual decision. He was adamant about not getting a vasectomy. And I felt I was getting up there in age. I did have an amniocentesis on both pregnancies, due to never having been pregnant in my early days, and also due to my older age. Much more risk for the baby's health is involved in older first-time mamas. My husband still says "I bet a 3rd baby would have been a baby girl". I quite disagree. I am almost positive a 3rd baby would have been another baby boy. After all, I immediately knew Matt was a boy. Three boys. Holy moly!

So by now, I am 36 yrs old. In five days, I turned 37. Christopher is already walking when he meets his baby brother. He never hit him or sat on him after

Matt was born. Once when I was pregnant with Matthew, I told Chris another baby was in mommy's stomach. He did hit my belly. Obviously he was too young to understand, but he did see the baby bump. It's Okay, Chris, Matt and I both forgive you!

We kept Matthew in a bassinet next to our bed, for a couple months, just like we did with Christopher. Eventually they were both in cribs. Both on bottles. Both in diapers. Both so totally dependent. And I potty-trained both at the same time. Plus the day Chris bit the top of his bottle nipple, I gladly swiped it away, and said "Look what you did! No more baba." He did not cry for it, simply adjusted to a sippy cup.

When Chris turned three, he was talking, but mostly just separate words. He was not forming sentences. His younger brother was just starting to talk, and he was forming sentences. I made an appointment with a speech therapist for Chris. We went to these appointments on a weekly basis for a number of months. His vocabulary started increasing and he started talking in longer sentences.

I continued to breast-feed Matthew when I returned to work at the prison.

Same procedure with the breast pump and ice chest. When I picked them up from the babysitter's, I would refrigerate the breast milk for his next day's feeding. Matthew also grew and was a wonderful baby. He slept pretty much the entire night. Again, we were blessed.

Chapter 29

When Matthew was only 2 months old, the four of us went camping. He slept above in an alcove, where a fourth person would sleep. Of course, he was not rolling over at this age. So he was content there. Daddy took one bed, which was converted from being a couch. Mommy and Christopher slept on another bed, which was converted from being the table. We even had a full bath tub. Not just a step-in shower, with the drain over the toilet area. Pure luxury and comfort. After carrying along playpen, diapers, baby clothes, a swing set, and food and drinks, all of this would go outside once we parked. For a number of years, Chris was contained in the crib, and Matt rested in the swing.

Our sons grew up on camping. They hiked, fished, played ball, went to the playground, went swimming. It was pure good, clean fun. After we took everything outside, all the toddlers paraphernalia, we had comfortable space inside the trailer. We even brought along a small color T.V., which is still working and is sitting on our kitchen counter, as I write this. We had a microwave too. A nice-sized refrigerator, and a stove top and oven. The full bath was the deciding factor when he purchased the trailer. Basically, all the comforts of home. I bathed the boys in the full bath, which was very convenient. Just like home.

However, I did need to turn off the T.V. in favor of using the microwave. We had already blown a fuse, while learning that just so much can be powered at the same time. The trailer had a heater, but we brought along a small electric heater. Less usage of propane.

Chapter 30

We travelled on one vacation to the mountains in the north part of the State. It was July and so hot, we were sweating at six in the morning. Mind you, we did not yet have air conditioning for the trailer. You betcha', when our vacation ended, we had an air conditioning unit installed on that roof. That was one of the best investments we ever made. That "baby" stayed on all day and night during our summer months of camping.

Our boys were three and four, and I continued to use daycare and working at the prison. It was so precious to pick them up after work, and both of them come running up to me with their arms raised. Pick me up! Pick me up! I miss those days when they were young. And that could be attributed to the fact that I am not yet a grandmother. Naturally, I want grandchildren. But I also so enjoy my adult relationships with both my sons. They have turned into good, mature, hard-working young men. No tattoos, no pierced lips, tongues, eyebrows, and other unmentionable parts of the body. They are gentlemen, and it shows.

Chapter 31

Back to their toddler days, it was November 7, 1987, and while I was at work, I fell down on the recently waxed floor. I blamed the inmates for using too much wax. Immediately upon falling, I felt a strong pain in my lower back. As the day progressed, I could not continue working. The pain increased in intensity. I went straight to the doctor, who said I probably pulled or strained a muscle in my back. Ok, here, I want you to realize, that turned out to be my very last day of going through those prison gates. The pain would not let up. It actually went down the outside of my right leg. By Christmas, I was going daily to a chiropractor. Even on Christmas day, and New Year's day.

Matthew developed the chicken pox, and Chris popped out with them a week later. Since I took the boys with me to the chiropractor, guess who also got the chicken pox? The young female chiropractor. She even had them on her face. I apologized profusely.

She took a couple weeks off, until the contact period ended. Her face was a disaster.

Poor sweet thing. She was very nice about it, though.

I was also going through a series of tests to determine the extent of injury. I continued to care for my babies. However, it was pretty difficult considering my pain. In January, the doctors analyzed a herniated disc, which would require surgery. If I chose not have surgery performed, I was likely to end up in a wheelchair. By then, I was barely walking. Just to wipe down the kitchen table became quite a task. And, remember, now, my babies were still young and needed me. By then, the daily visits to the chiropractor were deemed unnecessary. The first treatment I received was an ink injection in my back. I absolutely was not able to leave the hospital bed. One of the negative side effects was intense headaches. Well, here I was only to spend a few days in the hospital until my surgery a week later. They kept me that entire week, due to the fact that I had excruciating headaches. All together, I spent 23 days in the hospital. My folks took care of Chris and Matt. One day my folks brought the boys to visit me in the hospital. We went for a walk, me using the walker and just barely learning to walk again. I was holding on with both hands, when all of a sudden, Matthew started crying that he misses me and to "come home". He grabbed one of my arms, and I nearly lost my balance. He was crying, I was crying, Chris started crying. Holy cow! They just wanted me home. Poor babies.

I will tell you, that the next day after my surgery, they placed a potty chair next to my bed. The therapist helped me sit up, and stand on my feet. No easy accomplishment. When she told me to take a step away from the bed to the potty chair, I though I would die. I really thought I would never walk again. The healing process took months.

Chapter 32

After my lengthy stay in the hospital, I went to my folk's home to recuperate. The boys were also there. They were still too young for school. I remember I could not even lift a gallon-size milk bottle. We all stayed there for about a month, while my mom took care of me and the boys. Once I grew stronger, we went home. Thank you, mom! Besides that time, I could probably offer a zillion thank you's to both my mom and dad, for all their help the next few years.

The only positive thing that occurred after my surgery, besides staying home with my babies, was that I lost an incredible amount of weight. I actually went down to a size ten, a perfect size-ten, mind you.

Talking about weight, I did gain a lot of it back through the years. One time, I stopped all red meat for two years. Ate lots and lots of chicken. I actually had a dream, that I grew chicken feathers, under my armpits. No kidding!

Chapter 33

 I was super- protective of the boys when they were youngsters. They were allowed to play in the backyard only. The yard was completely fenced. One Christmas, we bought them a fort set. They played on the patio for hours. They even had "koon" hats and play rifles that we bought them, on one trip to an amusement park

When Matthew was 3 years old, and Chris 4 years old, they were riding out front on their scooters. I usually watched them from inside the house. For whatever reason, I realized Matt was no longer out front. So off Chris and I go to hunt up Matt. We found him at the neighborhood playground. He pedaled his little scooter, up the street, around the corner, onto a fairly much-driven street. He stayed on the sidewalk the entire time, thank you Lord. At least that is what he told me. Okay, so we walk up the street, my suspecting that is where he went. There he is. Happily playing on the bar set. When he saw me, he knew he was in big trouble. As I sit here, I enjoy writing about those times, but back then, I was furious.

These same little scooters, one time they were pedaling together, with a neighbor boy. They all three were almost on top of one another. Chris comes back with a bloody foot. His foot got caught between the scooters and did a fair amount of damage, looked like it almost ripped off his toe. Off to emergency again. Later when we returned home, I actually took a rag and small can of water, and wiped the blood off the sidewalk.

Chapter 34

So I am staying home with the boys. I had numerous doctor appointments to determine my eligibility to return to work. It was determined by my doctors, including State disability doctors, that my returning to the prison was not feasible. So in l988, I used up my sick time, and started getting a monthly pension. By then I had 23 years of State work, from 1965 to l988.

I healed slowly. We continued to go camping. I never got the nerve to drive the truck which pulled the trailer. The only time I got behind the wheel was to back it up to a camp site. With Rene' shouting directions and using hand signals. Comical, that is the only word to describe these attempts. Needless to say, we caught the attention of nearby campers who watched the whole scene. Probably laughing up a storm at our expense. I am not the most coordinated person. I do admit it! We decided to switch positions. The trailer needed to be straight and aligned with the hookups. It worked. We stopped being the highlight of the day for those nosy campers.

Chapter 35

Chris turned five and started kindergarten. We decided we wanted a larger home. We began looking in the area. After endless searching, we could not find our "dream house". We started going further East. There was a brand new tract. The sales office did not even have the floor plans available for inspection. Not even model homes available for access. Just a brief sketch of three models. We fell in love with a five bedroom 3 bath, 3 fireplaces, 3-car garage, two-story, Mediterranean style. We were able to leave the sales office, and walk to the location we wanted. We had choice as they were barely open. It was just a dirt lot. We put our house up for sale, and received an offer the very next day. Made a nice profit and applied most of the money to our new home. The only problem we encountered was my husband's drive to work. He would have to drive at least another hour. But he was willing to do that drive. So our house sold and closed escrow. Our new home was still not ready for delivery. We asked permission for garage access and explained our situation. The builder complied and we hired a moving van to move all our furniture and appliances and possessions into the garage. That left us without a home to live in. Well, wait a minute here, we had our travel trailer. So, I packed clothes for the boys and us, kept them in my truck, and we parked the trailer in the mountains. Rene' commuted to and from work, which was actually closer than our new home.

Christopher changed schools to the new school district and we drove down the mountain every day. Matt and I picked him up, after only ½ day for kindergarteners. Matt was only four and he stayed with me.

Rene' continued to drive down the hill and go to work. After nearly a month, our brand new home was ready for occupancy. It was necessary that I be very careful with lifting or moving anything heavy. My back surgery was not even one-year old.

The neighborhood became established and lots of families with children moved in. When the boys were about 7 and 8, I seemed to be the only stay-at-home mama. I took the State Daycare application and test, Rene' and I both were fingerprinted and background checks were conducted. Thus, my new occupation began. It was so nice because I was able to stay at home with my sons. Many times the school called me to pick up a sick child, that the mother had my name on-file for emergencies.

I went out and bought some used playpens, a high chair, plus car seats. It was 1990 and the income I received from this daycare proved very profitable. I saw at least four, one-baby families turn into two-baby families. In our family room, I completely covered the beautiful carpet with blankets. In the kitchen underneath the high chair, I placed an old tablecloth, because we all know babies make a mess and throw food on the floor. My very first daycare child was six months old. I even helped potty train her, and took her and the rest of the group to school in the morning, and then pick up the whole group after school. The reason I mention that little girl, blue eyes, was because she turned into a lovely young lady. She has already graduated from college. She was like my daughter that I never had. If my husband worked the graveyard shift, he would come home around 8 am, have breakfast, and sit down in the family room, and play with the babies.

My sons were boy scouts, enrolled in kung fu, and also participated in baseball and pee-wee football. We still went camping every summer and took off during weekends.

Chapter 36

One time when Matthew was three years old, we were at the camping site for a few days and dirty clothes piled up. I left the boys with my husband and went to the laundry room.

Rene' sat outside and read and was watching the boys. Well, you know how fast boys can take off before you even know it.

After the clothes were clean and folded, while I was walking back, my husband was carrying a sobbing, fully wet, Matthew. Both Chris and Matt had left the campsite and went to the pond. They both had removed their shoes and socks and placed them by the edge of the pond. Real neat-like. Matthew went into the water and waded out towards the middle, where it was the deepest. He started struggling and was attempting to keep his head above water. At three years old, he did not know how to swim. Christopher ran back to get their daddy and they both saved my baby's life. I dropped all the clothing I was carrying, and grabbed Matthew. He eventually quieted down, and went to sleep. To this day, as a young man, Matthew still has asthma, and I contribute that serious lung condition to his almost-drowning incident. Prior to his almost-drown, he never once experienced breathing difficulty. I believe the incident was more traumatic on him than I realized at the time.

When Christopher was seven, he had a very serious accident in the shower. I just know both boys were fooling around in the tub. Probably soaping up the tub and sliding around in it. That is my theory and I'm sticking to it! Matt yelled for me from upstairs. Chris showed me his bloody mouth. Apparently he acquired a hole between his lips and mouth area. An actual hole. It did stop bleeding that evening. So I did not think we needed to go to emergency. Well, let me tell you something. When we awoke the following morning, Chris' face was so swollen he was unrecognizable. It was like someone had placed a blown-up balloon inside his face. Yes, we hurriedly dressed and took off for the clinic. He was hospitalized for inflation of facial cellulites. Either myself or him must have kept sticking our hands inside his mouth, and, caused a severe infection. Chris spent a matter of days in the hospital and loved it. He had roommates and Nintendo. Plus, no homework.

Both boys attended the nearby elementary school. When Matt was six years old, he had a severe asthma attack and required hospitalization. Matt was the only one of our two sons, who sucked his thumb. Apparently being monitored and closely watched while he stayed in the hospital, convinced him to no longer put that thumb in his mouth. He actually stopped that childhood habit. Neither one of our boys ever sucked on a baby pacifier.

Rene' and I did not go out unless the boys went with us. When we did go to a restaurant, the whole family went. Everything was an entire family-affair. And I would not change that for anything. As I write this, so many memories from years past. And every single one I treasure, both good times and bad times.

One time, Chris and Matt were riding their bikes up the street. They returned and Chris showed me his right arm. He fell off his bike encountering an unseen small rock in the street. His arm was disfigured and the bone jutting out, near his elbow. Obviously, his arm was broken. He never once complained of pain. He wore that cast on his right arm for a few months, and learned to write with his left hand. Bravo for him!

Chapter 37

They were both baptized in the Catholic Church. My husband is Catholic and we both agreed we would raise our sons Catholic. The boys were around 10 and 9. I was receiving messages from our Lord to become a Catholic. For a year or so, I will admit that I continued to dwell on our Lord. Never, though, actually took the commitment. I did attend mass with our family. But I was not a true Catholic and sat through Mass, while the boys attended Sunday school.

The so-named "calling" to come to our Lord, became stronger. I called the Father at the local parish. He told me that the adult Catechism classes had already begun for that year. He told me he would take me under-his-wing. So, for two years, I went to an hour-talk with him every Tuesday evening. Since I was already baptized as a child, I did not need that sacrament. So, come Easter time, 1993, during the Easter vigil, I became a Catholic, during the evening Mass. Myself, along with the other students. I will forever be grateful for the opportunity to having spoken one-on-one with the Father.

The Father asked me where and when I was married. He said I needed to complete the marriage sacrament in the church. So in February 1994, the family was invited, along with our friends who attended our original wedding 15 years ago. Chris and Matt were able to see their mom and dad get married a second time.

Chapter 38

It is still early 1994, and I acquire an interest in real estate. Hey now, if that lady or that gentleman could do it, so can I!!! I enrolled in classes and started studying for the real estate agent exam. My husband was working the graveyard shift at the time. I would leave at 6 pm, after all the daycare children were picked up. The boys were fine because their daddy was at home, resting before he had to leave for work. I would get home around 9:30 pm, and then he would leave for his job. This goes on for a period of three months. I would study and repeat studying. I was fully prepared to take the state exam. And you know what folks, I actually passed on the first try. By June, I was hired at a local Real Estate office. But, initially it was basically part-time, because I was still doing daycare. Well, as any realtor knows, that just doesn't cut it. The job of a realtor requires full-time attention. So in August, I announced to the daycare mom and dad's that I was retiring my business. The boys were older and in junior high by now. Getting that first commission check was a killer. It took months and months, but eventually my real estate career escalated and it became very profitable.

The family still went camping. But the times available to just go off camping for the weekend, proved difficult. By now, the boys are involved in baseball and football. Matt turned out to be a darn-good player, and ended up in the baseball traveling team. Like one to two hours away.

They continue with their kung-fu classes. First getting the white belt, next the yellow belt, promoting to the brown belt. They went to different events to perform for the public. I am so proud to say that my boys received their black belts. They were the youngest, first ever, to receive their black belts from this 7th degree Black Belt Master. When they had classes, I would usually sit on the floor against one of the walls and just watch. Proud mama that I was. To this day, they tell me they have not forgotten some of their moves.

Chapter 39

It is early 1995. My being a realtor and all, one of our neighbors puts her house for sale with me. The husband received a job transfer to another State. During the Listing, the job transfer was cancelled, and we took their house off-the-market. She and I still talked occasionally. Their house had a spectacular view, was a different model than ours, still with five bedrooms, 3 baths, 3-car garage, three fireplaces. Just a bit of a different floor plan. With a catwalk at the top of the staircase, that looked down into the living room and dining room. We had a monster hot tub enough for 12 people in our own backyard. But this house had a pool and spa, with that marvelous view. Their backyard was wrought-iron fenced, and looked into a ravine. With only wildlife for company.

She calls me one day and announced that her husband received another job offer, yet in another State. I told her I might be interested in purchasing their home. They left to the other State for a few weeks and she gave me her house key, so I could show my family.

Their house had exactly the same colors as our current home. The master bedroom had blue accents just like ours. The rest of the house had window coverings that would match all our furniture. So, I put our house on-the-market, and it sold. We actually moved in, just across the street, on New Year's Eve. Those men from the moving company were so slow, that I told them to call the company and bring out a 3rd guy. After all, it was 6 pm on NYE. Didn't they want to go out and celebrate?

Chapter 40

It was summer l995. We took a mini-vacation to Catalina Inland. That was the very first time the boys spent time in a hotel. They were so excited. I mean after all, up till then, it was the trailer. We took pictures of them standing outside the door, and also inside by their beds. We were so close to the beach, I allowed them to walk there with their towels. It was a family vacation and we had a great time. Many of our vacations are forever a good solid memory.

The following year, we went camping for a couple weeks, around 4th of July. Halfway through that vacation, we had previously made plans to spend time at Disneyland. We spent five days there at the Disneyland Hotel. Just jump on the motor rail when we wanted to go to the park. I remember July 4th was on a Wednesday. It was our 3rd day there. The park was super-packed on that holiday. The four of us went swimming in the hotel's pool and we were the only ones enjoying the pool. There were people walking on an overheard walkway, looking down at us. It was heavenly. On Friday was our 5th day. None of us even wanted to go back to the park. We had literally seen it all. So we packed up, and headed to the mountains for the rest of that vacation.

I remember many swim parties at our home. Seems like every family had one or two boys, close in age, to my boys. Also, the boys would all gather at someone's cul-de-sac and play hockey for hours, each with their own hockey sticks, and they shared one of the netted goal and goalie equipment. They also played basketball. We had bought a huge net with attached apparatus which we turned onto its side, and rolled into the back gate. For appearance's sake, surely, not to hide it from theft. No one would be able to lift that "baby" onto a truck without having a diesel 18-wheeler roaring down our street.

The boys graduate from junior high to high school. Both continued to participate in sports. Christopher in football and wrestling. Matthew in football and baseball. I drove them to school in the morning, and if I had appointments scheduled in the afternoon, they took the school bus home. Chris studied for his driver's license and got his license when he turned 16. He was so involved in sports, sometimes getting home close to 10 pm or even 11 pm, wherever the game took place. I would drive over to the high school, and sit in the parking lot, waiting for the bus to bring the kids back. We bought him a used car, a Honda. After that, they drove to school together. Same thing, Matt got his driver's license the next year. One of my sellers moved out-of-state. She was going to donate her Toyota Camry to an organization. I bought it for $2000. Matt now also had a car. Listen here now, it is many years later, and if I knew what I know now, I would never have allowed them their own car. End of story! Absolutely, positively, no cars.

Chapter 41

By now, we seldom went out camping. With all the games and sports the boys were in, there was never a time to just take off. Our trailer was parked in a storage lot, was quite dirty and dusty, with four flat tires. One of our neighbors contacted us, and asked if we would consider selling the trailer. They saw it sitting there for months and knew we were not using it due to its negligence. It was great for hiding and storing Christmas presents. But, costly, due to paying storage fees. Our family talked it over, the other family got four new tires, and drove it off. We also had a campground membership, which was also costly, paying quarterly dues, and this same couple, bought the membership from us too. I do not miss the work involved in camping. But I do thank the Lord for all the special times we shared while camping.

One time it was raining, and the four of us sat around the table playing Uno, or playing Old Maid. Those times are so memorable and precious. Or we would sit together, and watch an old video we brought along.

The boys also originally learned trick-or-treating, going from campsite to campsite. They never trick or treated in our neighborhood until they got older.

Chapter 42

My dad, besides having this blood cancer, had a couple of strokes. He kept contracting pneumonia. It was agreed between my folks and me that they wanted to make me their executor. During one of my visits, I brought a "Power of Attorney" form and all three of us went to a Notary Public. We also went to the city offices and had the POA recorded.

The boys are in high school and it is the late 1990's. Rene's dad has had major heart surgery, plus an amputated leg due to his diabetes, over the last few years. He was deteriorating fast. I somehow ended up also taking care of his folks.

In late 1999, I took him for a doctor appointment. He already had been in and out of the hospital. Beside his heart condition (a pacemaker was placed under his chest skin) and his diabetes, the doctor diagnosed pancreatic cancer. It was early January 2000. His sugar level was in the 400's (toxic) and he was weakening from the cancer. He ultimately remained in the hospital till he died.

And here I was still running back and forth for my folks. Besides that, Rene's mom needed surgery in the early part of 2000. I got up at 4 am and picked her up. I took her to the hospital. She was released the same day. Not a super-serious surgery.

While Rene's dad spent the remainder of his life in the V.A. hospital, I am of the opinion we was well-cared for. Except that he told me he was getting only peanut butter sandwiches for lunch. I located the doctor and told him we needed to discuss this with the dietician. From then on, he received full meals. The doctor called me in April at 5 pm, and told me to come down to the hospital. It was time. He would likely not last the night. Now I want ya' all to know that my mother-in-law spoke mostly Spanish, with only a few words in English. And I hardly knew any Spanish. So, I called my mother-in-law and told her, "we need to go to the hospital". She said, "no, it is late and she was tired". I somehow communicated to her that: "I am on my way to pick her up regardless." She was in denial, you see. She was preparing the house for his return, and for Easter. She also refused to believe that his leg would be amputated, when the deed was done a number of years back.

Chapter 43

A couple incidents happened while the family waited in his room. The next morning sometime around 6 am, I remember Chris and me standing near his bed, their grandma on the other side, and my husband and Matt, leaning against the wall directly facing the bed. My father-in-law asked us: "who is that tall man dressed in white, standing there"? He pointed to the very same wall where Rene' and Matt were standing. They both whipped their heads around. Of course, no one was there that we could see. Rene' told his dad "Dad, no one is there". He disagreed saying "he has been waiting a long time". Do you have faith? I do, and this just confirmed it all the more.

He was on an auto-drip of morphine. Later in the morning, he was hot and we took turns fanning his face. That apparently contented him. He had his eyes closed, and was very near death. He tried to lift his body, at the same time, clapping his hands together in pure delight and joy, and his eyes glowed. We asked him what he saw, and he told us "you are bothering me" and to "stop disturbing me". Within about two hours, he died. Again, faith in our Lord, you gotta believe.

Since my mother-in-law did not drive, I somehow got delegated to drive her to numerous doctor appointments, the dentist (like 10 times), the optometrist, the hearing specialist, to get hearing aids. This did not include trips to the bank, trips to the grocery store, and, as a family, we took her to Sunday mass. Apparently our extended family did not consider my real estate career as a job. To put it bluntly, I was overwhelmed. Here I was on-call for my dad, my mother-in-law, my own family had concerns and issues.

Chapter 44

In 2002, she went to live with her other son. I am most grateful, because that was the start of many surgeries, between 2002 and today 2010. My dad was 89 and continued to live at home, using a cane, not his walker. He must have fallen at least five times, before I finally started making inquiries about nursing homes. So, in 2003, the hospital found a facility close to their home, and they called to tell me they had a bed available. I was like driving out weekly to my folks. One time, my mama called me, and said "papa is in the hospital". I automatically went home from work, and packed an overnight bag. Drove straight to their hospital. Another stroke.

Getting back to the nursing home that had a bed available for my daddy. I told my mom what was happening, and she approved because she couldn't sleep, always afraid of him falling down. I remember sitting down in their den, just me and daddy. This is so difficult to write. I began by telling dad that because of all his falls, and actually getting hurt, mind you, I found a bed for him in a nursing home. Forever more, I will see his face. He was beyond shock. It hurt me too. He was my "daddy" and I was making a rough decision concerning his welfare. He accepted without much argument. One of the hardest decisions I have ever made. Forgive me, Daddy?

Chapter 45

Chris had graduated and moved into an apartment with some of his buddies. It was 2001, 9/11, when my Matthew woke me up and told me to hurry and watch the T.V. news. Terrorist attacks on our twin towers. Lord, how could this be happening in the United States? As we watched the one tower burning, the second tower was attacked. All those poor souls. And the rest of the people crazily running about the streets of New York. Choking on all the debris flying around the city. It reminded me of a dream I had previously. There was a massive huge, green frog, on a city street, spitting out fire from his mouth. When I compare my dream of that ugly frog with 9/11, I see it correlates with one another.

Basically, everyone besides my direct family, were taken care of. I continued working as a realtor. It was May of 2002. Just two days prior, I went to the doctor complaining of lower back pain. Little did I realize, I nearly died. So on Wednesday, I spent most of the day in bed. My back and stomach were in horrible pain. My husband needed to get up at 3:30 in the morning for work. It was around 10 pm and my son Chris was watching television. I dressed and went down the stairs, and told him to take me to emergency. I did not want to disturb my husband, thinking we would be back in two hours or so.

Chapter 46

In emergency, the doctors took x-rays and found a hole in my stomach. Food was leaking out and going everywhere. This was quite fatal. The doctors called it a perforated stomach. They performed emergency surgery and I was out of it for days.

While my family came to visit me in my room, I even told them to get out, blaming them for my ulcerated stomach. I have since apologized. Heavily sedated, you know. It had nothing to do with raising teenagers? Stress and nerves were a daily habit with raising two healthy teenagers? Okay, guys, I am sorry.

I was released on a Friday. My sister Manya picked me up from the hospital. We drove to my house for some clothes, and went to spend my recuperation at mom and dad's house. Actually I did not wear a bra for over a month. I was opened up from the bottom of my breast line to my naval. And the bottom of the bra would have irritated my wound, which was closed up with staples.

So, we finally arrive at my folks. I was totally drained and exhausted. My sister prepared a spaghetti dinner. I got out of bed and sat at the kitchen table, eating a small bit. I was extremely tired and left to take a shower. Finished, I got out of the shower, and while I was drying off with a towel, my stomach started churning.

I yelled for my sister. I threw up my dinner. It was red, and I assumed it was the spaghetti sauce. I was shaking too from throwing up. But upon closer examination, the vomit was blood. Lots and lots of blood. Clots and all. My sister called my house to let my family know. My mom and my sister drove me to emergency. The receiving nurse actually asked me "Are you normally this pale"? Apparently I turned white. I was also scared. What was happening here, anyhow? I was shivering uncontrollably. Total count, they placed eight blankets on me. Looking back, I realize I was "in shock". They stuck a tube down my throat, while telling me to keep drinking the water, so that the tubing would slide down. I remember having that down my throat for a couple days. When I was taken in the wheelchair for tests, I felt like an elephant. With that thing unplugged and hanging, I thought it looked just like an elephant's trunk .

Sometime the next evening, I woke up and saw that they were giving me blood transfusions. I must have thrown up a lot of blood. I was very sick. I remember using the potty chair next to my bed, while nurses were drawing yet more blood samples. In that situation, you lose all humility. My family and mother-in-law came to visit me. It was so good to see my family. Remember now, this was back-to-back hospitalizations. When I was released from the hospital, I returned to my mom and dad's house.

Chapter 47

Eventually I returned home and started my real estate business. Forevermore, I will remember hearing my sons' friends running up and down the staircase. If I happened to be out of bed, usually I still had on my nightgown. Bad bed hair and all. These young boys would just say, "Hello Mrs. Loera". They knew I was not feeling well.

Chris is still living with his buddies and Matt is living at home. They were one year apart in school, so while Matt finished his high school education and received his diploma, Chris and two of his buddies took off for Europe. I seriously questioned this vacation, after all, America was under terrorism. They travelled by train and backpack though London, France and a few other countries. They travelled light, spending little money.

It was a great experience for these three young men.

It is the year 2003, when I coughed. I felt a lump stick out on my stomach. Off again I go to the hospital. My doctor did, indeed, conclude it was a hernia. He just conveniently had an opening for surgery the next day. So I went home and prepared my family for another surgery. Went to the bank, withdrew money, and went to the grocery store to buy supplies. After surgery, he told me he repaired not one, but two, hernia's. He also inserted a 4 by 6 net on my stomach lining, to prevent any other outbursts. Another full week's stay for me.

Chapter 48

That year, I also found a small growth behind my right ear. I went to the ENT (ear, nose and throat specialist). I followed through with some testing, and the doctor told me it was a tumor, because over a couple of month's time, he was measuring it. He told me it was necessary to perform surgery to remove it. I questioned another surgery, but the doctor was adamant. I told him "just leave the tumor", and, of course, that was not possible. It would only continue to grow and become malignant. So later that year, I had a same-day surgery. Lord, how they wrapped me up. I truthfully believe nurses had a contest on which patient left with the highest turban-wrapped head. My head was wrapped up in surgical tape, with a drainage cup by the wound. At the top, it was tied up into three knots. Yes, three knots! I was pathetic-looking. My sons came to pick me up when I was discharged, and all they could do was stare at me.

When I was wheeled out, I looked down. I did not want to see anyone. I was so embarrassed. I kept that thing on for three days. It was unbearable. Also, the gauze was wrapped around my throat and it was extremely uncomfortable. Naturally, there is a photo of me with that gross thing on my head. But the good news was the tumor was benign.

For years now, following my back surgery, I have needed a cane to walk, mostly for stability, and also for my right knee. I had extreme arthritis in my knee, among other parts of my body. Even though I had L4/L5 back surgery, I also since acquired degenerative discs in my back. For a couple of years, I was getting cortisone injections in my knee. It did help for a little while. It is 2004 when I had a scope- type surgery on my knee. Same-day surgery, again. The doctor took pictures of my knee, and showed my husband and me – where he cleaned up the arthritis as best as he could. They looked like flowing feathers.

Chapter 49

The following year in 2005, I had breast reduction surgery. This was performed to remove the heaviness plus the small fat cells. Excruciating recovery. This surgery was, in reality, a personal choice, not like my other do -or -die surgeries.

I continued to visit my daddy in the nursing home. I asked my mom if daddy had all his clothes for his funeral. White shirt, white sash, white pants, and white shoes. She showed them to me, which was devastating. I knew where these clothes would end up. On my daddy! Don't forget now, the whole Russian tradition. He was in and out of the hospital on numerous occasions. He had pneumonia and was coughing up blood. One hospital stay, I had to wear a hospital gown, cap, and gloves. He was in isolation. A tuberculosis caution. Which he did not have. I remember seeing him spit a blood colt into a cup. I was the only one in his room, and I thought, oh Lord, my poor daddy. When he got better, he was returned to the nursing home. He was losing weight and was very tired. He used to wheel around the home and stop to chat with his friends. I was visiting him weekly and could see his descent. No longer was he riding around. Even his interest in reading the newspaper and watching T.V. disappeared. He started napping all day long and did not even dress for the day. My sister Manya called me on October 9th. She said: "Papa doesn't look good". So off I go to the nursing home.

Chapter 50

I drove out and picked up my mom first, and the two of us go see daddy.

Yes, he does not look good at all. I asked him: "Did the doctor see you yet today?"

He told me "yes". From his looks, I felt he should be hospitalized again. So I went in search of the facility doctor. I found her at another station, working with a nurse. I told her: "I understand you had seen my dad earlier", and that "I felt his condition required hospitalization". She agreed to look at him again. So, I returned to my dad's room and waited for her. She did show up in a relatively short time. She spoke and examined my dad and decided he should be transported to emergency. I want you all to know that my dad was a joker, always telling tales and jokes. Corny ones, and, I miss them to this day. I told dad that the EMT was going to take him to the hospital. He joked and said he was going in-style. While dad was transported to the hospital, I took mom home so she can rest. She was not well herself, being 88 yrs old. We both had a fast bite of cheddar cheese with some bread. She laid down and I then proceeded to emergency. I stayed with my daddy until he was placed in a room late that night

In the meantime, my sister stopped by. By now, the doctors told us our dad was indeed at the end of his life. His lungs just could not survive much longer. Mind you, he has been on antibiotics for a couple of years and his total resistance was down.

Sometime after my sister left, I realized dad was either in a coma or feel asleep. He was not responding to my questions. I went up to my dad, and his mouth was wide open, probably desperately trying to breathe. My dad had a full white beard, once again. I look at him closely, and discover a white hair in his mouth, from his beard (bradhdaa). I told my daddy that I was going to take out that piece of beard. He just absolutely could not go meet Jesus with hair in his mouth. Okay now, how am I going to do this? I did not want to just stick my hand in his mouth. So I looked around and saw the sink. There I got a paper towel and wet it with water. I went back to my dad and successfully removed that piece of white beard from his mouth. He never woke up and I apparently did not disturb him.

To this day, I try to remember when my daddy and I stopped speaking. I knew my daddy was dying, yet, I do not remember the exact sequence of events that occurred that day. I sat with him, alone, all day, until he was assigned a room. As I mentioned earlier, I went up with him until he was comfortably placed in a bed. It was just after midnight, and I left to go to their house to sleep.

Chapter 51

My sister was in charge of calling our extended family, and the preacher. The next morning, we all went to the hospital. Throughout the day, relatives also visited.

I remember talking to my dad, whispering in his left ear that I was so, so very sorry for the times I was not a good daughter.

The church preacher had not visited as of yet. It was sometime around 4 pm. My uncle stood at the front of daddy's bed and said a prayer in Russian. There must have been eight or ten of us standing around the bed. The Russian folk then proceeded to sing a couple of Russian songs. My dad did indeed look to stir a bit. Perhaps the singing somehow entered into his brain. He looked content and quite peaceful. Of course, we closed his open mouth.

I remember two nurses coming into the room, to change his bedding, diaper, and hospital gown. We moved to the front of the room to allow my daddy some discreet privacy. I remember hearing him moan every time they turned him. That will forever be the last I heard of his voice

By that time, mom was totally exhausted. So, I told my sister and her daughter to stay with daddy, and I was taking mom home to rest. I made sure she was laying down, when the phone rings close to 5 pm. My niece called on her cell phone, while daddy was very near death. As she was talking to me, I was able to share his last breath. Thank you, Sarah, dear.

It was October 10, 2005, and I immediately went to wake mom because she did fall asleep. Bless her. I sat on the side of her bed and took her hands in mine. I took a deep, strangled breath, and told her daddy is "gone". We both cried, and I told her to get dressed. We needed to go back to the hospital.

Once again, prayers were said. The preacher had arrived by this time. Most left to go home, but my uncle was adamant I stay and wait for the undertaker. It was Russian tradition, that the deceased not be removed and taken to the hospital basement (where most hospital morgues are located). So my sister and mom went home, while my niece and I stayed with my daddy. The Russian mortuary was contacted and we waited for them to come get my daddy. By now, it has been several hours. Sometime around 9 pm, two men arrived and placed a nametag of my daddy's right foot and also one on his right hand. Did I watch? Yes, I was transfixed by the scene. And, next, they zipped up a body bag on my dad's form. My niece and I continued to watch, until they wheeled him out into the corridor, to a different elevator used for the deceased. Lord have mercy, if you are waiting for an elevator, and when it opens, there is a body in a body bag. That just cannot happen. You just might, possibly, end up in the same condition. So, she linked arms with me, and we walked to the other elevator and went home.

Chapter 52

The next morning, I took my dad's burial clothes to the dry cleaners. To have them pressed and ready later that same day. I stopped at the local florist and bought two funeral arrangements, one from my mom, and one from his children and great-grand-children. I also went to the Russian mortuary, to complete last-minute paperwork. In case you are wondering, Yes, the staff did try, and I repeat, try, to sell me something more expensive. Note I call it the Russian mortuary. But it is basically a mortuary for all the public. It simply became used by the Russians, due to the courtesy of the staff.

During the actual funeral procession from church to cemetery, they courteously wear the white Russian shirt and sash, same as worn by the Russian men.

By now, my daddy's burial clothes were ready to pick up. I hung them up in the closet. Then I drove home to prepare my own white clothes and that of my husband and sons.

It was Friday evening, and Lord, I was drained. The funeral was scheduled for Tuesday October 14 at 11 am. I had adequate time until Monday at 4 pm when we take his body to church. And, thankfully, time to rest. I had hardly no sleep since Thursday, when I rushed to the nursing home.

Chris and Matt were no longer living at home. They shared a two-bedroom apartment about 15 minutes from our home. That weekend, we prepared two sets of white clothing. Remember, now, one set for pre-burial, and another complete clean set for after burial services. I knew my folk's home would be full of overnight guests. So the four of us rented a hotel suite for two nights. For Monday night and Tuesday night. The boys travelled in one of their own cars. Along about 3 pm, after we settled into our room and got dressed in our first set of white clothing, we went to pick up mom, and proceeded to go to the mortuary. At 4 pm, we all went into their chapel, where daddy was laying on a table.

Same conditions as when my sister Nadia, died. After we approved his dress and his beard and hair, they picked him up and placed him in the all-white coffin. Daddy's coffin was put in the hearse, and we all travelled to church. The Russian relatives and church members began arriving throughout the evening. Us close to daddy sat on wooden benches on both sides of the coffin. My husband sat at the head, as he was the eldest male in our family, me and mama, then our two sons. Directly in front on us sat Jason, my nephew, and his mom, and my niece Sarah. Since the time my sister died in 1973, these benches provided for us included a back rest. But, no slouching, no crossing your legs, always sit prim and proper. For hours and hours! Remember, now, those old biddies were notorious for gossip. If I even attempted to cross my legs, I would get the "look". Only the immediate family took off to the kitchen in groups of 3-4, and had a dinner of soup, bread, hot tea, chocolate candy and fresh veggies and fruit. Thank you, Tanya, for preparing that meal. She is a close family friend of the family, dating back to our farm days.

After the 8 pm prayers, people started to leave the church. We, naturally, stayed on till midnight. The preacher stayed on till 10 pm. He handed my husband the church keys in order to lock up. To me, that was the greatest compliment I could ever receive from these Russian people. They have changed their religious beliefs over the last 30-40 years. It would have been unheard of in the 60's and 70's to trust my "nin-nash" husband with the church keys. So we placed the lid of the coffin to cover my daddy, inserting four bibles at each end to circulate the air. We safely locked up the church and left my daddy in there all alone. Gone were the days of an all-night vigil. Our family did chose this option because we were all so very exhausted and needed a couple hours sleep. I do believe some of the Russian families continue to remain with the body all night. But the next day is the burial, and another full day from early morning to late at night.

Chapter 53

We took mom home and then the four of us went to our hotel. Mom and dad's house was packed with family. We showered and tried to sleep. I set the alarm for 6 am. Before we all knew it, the alarm went off. We dressed in the same white clothing. Obviously we had clean, new underwear. Naturally, the men wore dark pants, with a white shirt. No tie. You will soon learn the significance of wearing the same clothing for the burial. Why we were prepared with two separate sets of white clothing.

We took off to pickup my mom. There was a light drizzle. We arrived at the church around 7 -8 am. We removed the coffin lid; and, there lay my daddy. Fresh tears all over. We had a bag of fresh small, beautifully embroidered hankies. All white for the men, and white with embroidered colorful edging for the women. The kitchen staff soon arrived to prepare the four-course feast. The preacher and congregation started coming in and were singing Russian songs and, prayers began at 11 am. I must tell you that since I married a "nin-nash", I was basically kicked out of the church. Over the years, when I went to a Russian funeral for one relative after another, I was allowed to sit by the coffin, but never allowed to participate in the final prayers, where the coffin is moved to the front of the church and everyone kneeled and prayed besides the coffin. Yet another miraculous change in their religious heritage! My family and my niece (who married "nin-nash") were allowed to escort my daddy to the front. Some time earlier, we had decided on six pallbearers. Some confusion arose when six of the younger Russian men took my daddy's coffin outside the church, to be placed in the hearse. Hold on here, what about my two sons, one of his other grandsons, and my three nephews? While daddy went into the hearse, we were explained that while in church, it was necessary for only Russian men to take him outside. Understand here, that I consider this Russian population a bit Amish. Even the men and women sit separately during prayers. Once the feast is presented, tables and benches are put together, and everyone then sits together. Which, mind you, is yet later this same day.

We all get into our cars and follow the funeral procession to the cemetery. My mom chooses my husband to take her in her wheelchair. No easy task, being that he was pushing her on grass, with many holes. The grave site in the ground has already been dug out.

A shade awning was placed above for protection from rain or sun. Earlier it was misty but by now, noon time, it dissipated. Our choice of pallbearers carried daddy to his last resting place. The lid was carried by two younger male members of the family. I believe cousins. I cannot remember. We assembled as close as possible to the coffin. While Russian songs were sung and last prayers said, the lid was slowly placed on top of daddy.

I remember bending down as he started to disappear. We were standing at the front of his body. They lowered the lid in back first and then it came down in front. I kept bending further and further down, for my last look of my wonderful daddy. I said "No, No daddy".

I leaned over to my mom in her wheel chair and sobbed. A shovel was filled with dirt and passed around for the immediate family to get a handful of dirt and throw it onto the coffin as it was being lowered into the ground. The Russian people continue to sing their lovely songs. Once the coffin is lowered six feet, the three heavy straps are lifted up, if successfully, if not, one or so stayed behind. Seems to me they left one. It does not matter. Most Americans funerals, the people then leave. Not so with the Russians. The young men start taking turns shoveling the dirt in the grave. Never mind they are wearing dress shoes. When the deed is done, we leave. The day is not over.

Chapter 54

The four of us go to our room, rest as much as possible, and then shower and change into our 2nd set of clean white clothes. Okay, you are most likely wondering about the significance of this ritual. Whoever was sitting next to the deceased, were considered unclean, their clothing that is. Thus, the shower and change of clothing. I made sure we all were ready for the evening event. Even though I was literally kicked out of the Russian church, I took their values to heart. After all, that was the way I was raised, and I would never disappoint my mom.

Again, we left our hotel room and picked up my mom. Poor sweetheart! She was so very tired, and she just lost her husband of 70 years. We head to the church in a caravan. Another niece and nephew (Andrea and John) were resting at mom and dad's. They had come earlier to daddy's burial. Church services began at

5 pm, and prayers at 6 pm. Always, prayers for the deceased and beautiful Russian songs. Between 7 and 8 pm or so, the men moved benches and started placing tables together, (actual long wooden planks resting on two sawhorses. And benches placed on both sides. White tablecloths overlapped each other. The four-course meal began with songs, which were sung between the courses. Since I was a child, only a small variation of this meal has changed. The first course included hot tea, fresh vegetables, like lettuce, cucumbers and tomatoes. Sugar cubes, not the granulated type either, dates and lemons. The second course was "Lapsha" (a thick egg-noodle soup prepared from lamb or beef). Oh yes, always bread and salt remained on the table. This constituted our Lord. Similar to communion in the Catholic faith. Onto the 3rd course, it consisted of a large plate filled with the meat that was prepared earlier for the soup. And, lastly, the 4th course was always whatever fruit was in season, whether it was apples and oranges, or perhaps watermelon and cantaloupe. This was served family-style. The food was placed on the tables, every few feet or so. More than plenty for everyone seated.

When the feast ended, the men took apart the tables and benches, where they stacked them neatly against the wall. While the cleaning staff were washing dishes and cleaning up the kitchen, a last prayer and songs were sung. By now, it is close to 10 pm.

It is over. My daddy is gone. I loved him so very, very much. I sit here shedding tears by the bucketful.

Ironically, today is Father's day 2010. I continually stop typing to wipe my eyes. Daddy, I dedicate this book to you, in addition to my own family. And thank goodness for Microsoft Word. I can simply hit "save" and return later. Which, I have been doing the last couple of months.

Before we left the church, I had to settle the various payments for the church usage, janitorial services, the lady who baked the bread, launder services, the whole complete food bill, and this amounted to a lot, considering feeding close to 200 people.

Chapter 55

My sons decide to drive back home that night. We all went back to the hotel and they picked up their items and suitcases. Not so for my husband and me. There is still more responsibilities that I must do. The next day, after a relatively good sleep, we headed to the nursing home. Sometime during the previous days, I had notified the facility of dad's death. They told us we needed to come in and pick up his possessions. We went through his stuff and donated all his clothes to the facility. After all, there are many patients who have absolutely no family visit them. They are simply taken to the home, and forgotten.

In every nursing home, not just that one. Truly sad. But many of these patients have Alzheimer's, dementia, or other ailments which make them appear quite loony. I remember men patients in their wheelchairs trying to grab me. Or some women carrying on, crying and all, another one yelling, "This is hell. Am I in hell?" You gotta chuckle here. It is so pathetic but true. And, ya all know, many of us will be there someday.

When we left the nursing home, we took daddy's bag that we collected, and went back to my folk's house. We had earlier checked out of our room. During the next couple of weeks, I had lots of phone calls to make. Social security, so they can stop my mom's benefits and convert to dad's benefits, my dad's health plan, their bank account, and then once I received his Death Certificate, distributing them.

Chapter 56

It is late 2005, and I continue working in real estate. Earlier I mentioned the boys had moved out. No way would they live at home when they can have all the freedom they want. Away from Me. In all fairness, they are my babies, and always would be my babies. They gave me a book one year, "Love You Forever". To this day, I am pathetic when I read the story. I sob all over the place. A real tear-jerker for mommy's. It is still 2005, Thanksgiving time. We picked up my mom and brought her to our home. Even though the boys moved out, we never even considered moving ourselves. It was a huge home, but what the heck, it was "home". It is Sunday morning, and we three are sitting in the kitchen/family room combo, my husband and me reading the Sunday newspaper. We both saw a single-story, in our very own city, for sale, at a reasonable price. We asked mom if she would consider living with us. Understand here, I am not yet well, but I would do anything, absolutely anything, for my mom. She was 88 years old and starting to use a wheelchair. I showed my mom the newspaper photo and, just like that, on the spot, she and I get dressed and leave to preview this home. It was a senior, gated community, and I was just 57 years old, so we would be eligible to purchase one of their homes. Mom and I drove around with the saleslady. Mom used her walker for this trip. Naturally, I fell in love with the model home, which was the last of that floor plan available. It had a front-street kitchen view, a living area, and, thank you Lord, a formal dining area. Two bedrooms, the master with a Jacuzzi tub, all righttt! The third bedroom was converted to a den. Well, let me tell you, all the homes since this one, my husband always had his own den. And, this was just too perfect! Built-in shelves for a bookcase and assorted shelving. In a gorgeous wood with thick beveled glass inserts. The entry to the den included double-French doors. Rene' was going to fall in love with this room. Sure enough, we tell the lady we will be back. We rush home and eagerly discuss this with Rene'. It also included an oversized 2-car garage, with a patio attached to the house, concrete slab and awning, included . The kitchen was designed for the elderly and handicapped. Pull-out drawers, with a kitchen island. By then, we already owned two houses with kitchen islands. So off we go, with our checkbook, nat. This time, my mom stayed behind to take an afternoon nap. We were able to get the keys from the saleslady because she was with other prospective buyers. Well you guessed it, folks, he also fell in love with the house. Now my being a realtor and all, I knew the pitch that saleslady was giving us. About there being two other interested couples, for the same house. So, without more prompting, we signed a contract and gave her a deposit for $10,000. Back then, my real estate career was booming. Plus, we had enough equity in our house, to take out a second, so that we can buy our new home in cash. I put our current home on-the-market. It sold for an astronomical price. So, actually we owned two homes at the same time. When escrow closed on our old home, we never even needed to make a payment on the 2nd deed. So, goodbye to our huge dream home and welcome our retirement home. We all will miss that backyard. I remember sitting in the spa or pool, and watching fireworks on 4th of July. And the birds! They were in birdy-heaven because we had a gigantic birdfeeder attached to the wrought-iron fencing.

Chapter 57

It is early Spring, 2006. We had a bedroom all prepared for my mom. I put up pretty lacey drapes in her room. Rene' and I took our time moving, actually setting up the kitchen and bathrooms. We also took numerous trips, moving our clothes into the closets. Rene' had moved most of the garage stuff into our new garage. Not including the heavy workbenches. We actually moved in prior to our other house closing escrow. It proved to be the most easiest move ever. I went back to our huge home to have the carpets professionally cleaned, as I had promised the buyers I would. Cost like $500.

Mom and I went to her doctor to discuss a hospital bed. We had both bathrooms equipped with handicap rails inside the bath and toilet areas. My sister was currently taking care of my mom, except for legal and banking issues. My mom simply changed her mind about moving in with us. She wanted to remain close to her Russian people. She kept crying and crying. We told her that we would never pressure her, and she can come to visit. So now I sit in her bedroom, with the pretty lace curtains, and write this book at the computer. Also, my real estate business in conducted in this same room.

In the Russian tradition, a memorial service takes place a year after the dearly departed.

The year 2006 continues. Both my sons are working and continue to live together. Something their dad could never understand. Probably, partly due to the fact that his older brother and him do not get along. Still. They had two completely different set of friends.

I have to compare by sons to their dad and uncle. Before Chris and Matt moved out, it seems like I was constantly pulling them apart, when they would start to wrestle. We had a female Dalmatian, named Dolly, and both she and I would prance and dance around those two, she barking, me yelling, the boys yelling and grunting.

Chapter 58

So it is approaching October. The first anniversary of my daddy's death. Again, I make arrangements with the church and my aunt and uncle, who were helping me. The same church procedures, takes place, with prayers, songs, and the four-course feast. I went alone this time. It is really intimidating to people their first time. My mom, by now, was in a wheelchair. She turned 89 in 2006. She was under a lot of medication and it was completely noticeable that she had developed dementia. My sister was living with her and taking care of her. I remember one weekend or week that I picked up my mom, to stay with us, for a few days. After one of her naps, she told me that there was a fat, fully plucked, duck, in my refrigerator, all ready for a soup. Ya' just gotta agree with people who have dementia. She would cry and tell me "How come no one told me daddy died?" That was a hard one to answer. Sometimes she would refer to my sister as two of them.

Other times, she would ask me" Who hired that lady"? One time when my daddy was still alive and living at the nursing home, mom and I drove there to visit. When we left, she told me that daddy wanted her to move in with him "So he can get a little". True stories, all of them.

Chapter 59

So it is late 2006, and I realize my mom is becoming too much of a burden for my sister to take care of. I, myself, can barely walk some days due to arthritis in my back, hips, and knees. Not to mention both hands and left shoulder. Okay, so it is time to once again make a difficult decision. I talk with mom's doctor and she agreed with me that I should locate a nursing home. I chose a different nursing home this time, actually closer to her home. The home my dad was in was selected by the hospital, during one of his accidents. I visited this home and, was as pleased as one could be, considering the circumstances. They called me on December 26th and told me they had a bed available.

I called my sister and told her of my decision. The next day, my husband, oldest son Christopher, and myself went to pick up mom. When we took her to our car, I told her, in Russian, to sit down. "Seddze". She started pulling down her pants, as if to go to the bathroom. I told her "newt" (No). I never once told her where she was going. She was assigned to a room of three. I told her she was in a hospital where she will be taken good care of.

For the first couple of days they strapped my mom to the wheelchair. They did not want her to fall out, or get up and fall down. This was totally unsatisfactory to me! I complained to the staff and they stopped the strapping. My mom could still walk, although slowly, and with an aide of sorts. She was one very unhappy camper. She refused to eat for days. Now next is something I am not proud to say, but she said "You guys treat me just like a dog". She really meant a dog gets old, and dies. But what she said hurts to this day. I love my mom very much. She eventually did adjust, and moved to another quieter room. One of her old roommates played her television full-blast. When we went to visit mom, we had to ask that lady very nicely to turn down her TV.

We were visiting her every 3 or 4 weeks. And, miraculously, her state-of-mind improved. I deposited money on-the-books for her to get her hair washed and styled weekly. She even has her nails clipped every once-in-awhile. Her disposition changed, to where she got used to the place and must have realized this was now home.

Chapter 60

It became 2007. I had discussed with my sister long ago, that I would put mom and dad's house for sale, in the event they no longer lived in it. Needless to say, our sisterhood was damaged. I actually mourned the loss of another sister. I completely closed-up and stayed in bed for a week. In was in April, that their home closed escrow.

My arthritic condition continued to worsen. I still worked in real state, and the market fell to a pitiful down period. Lenders tightened their loan commitment policy and many buyers were just not qualified to purchase a home. After selling my folks house, my production in real estate continued to decline.

During the fall of 2007, I was tested, poked, and further poked. I went for acupuncture a few months. Did not really think this method of pain elevation worked. So, I stopped going.

Chapter 61

During the summer of 2008, my mother-in-law was hospitalized. She was 93 years old. Her health continued to worsen. She had a stomach infection that no amount of antibiotics worked. She was released to a nursing home. In August, the family was called together and she was moved to a single room, to allow our family privacy. She went into a coma and survived for almost a week. Rene' and I were with her, plus the hospice nurse, at the time she died. This hospice nurse was very astute and was excellently trained. We three gathered around her bed and joined hands, saying "The Lord's Prayer". Her face seemed to change expression, one of peace. God bless you, Luisa. Her funeral took place days later, and she was rested forevermore, above her husband at the cemetery. Thank you Sally and Laura, the assigned hospice nurses. You two did a fantastic job!

Chapter 62

It was May of 2008. My oldest son Christopher studied for his real estate license and, once he got his license, was working with me. I saw a new condo listing that would be affordable for my sons. Actually with the rent they were paying, their mortgage payment plus association fee, would save them around $300 to $400 a month. We both went to look at the condo. It is in a gated-community, a super-plus, and the condo was upstairs, with a massive balcony, all on top of their two-car garage. They both qualified and, thus, became homeowners in July. It was actually closer to us. To this day, I have not returned to their home, because of my legs. As for them, they are most likely eternally grateful that I do not visit. I am always asking them "Do you guys clean your toilets, the kitchen, the bath tubs?" After all, for years we have always had a housecleaner. They should want to go home to a clean house. So far, I have no idea what their place looks like. Just as well.

Chapter 63

By April of 2009, I was in a wheelchair. I just could not walk any longer. The pain in my knee was horrendous. We had a family vacation scheduled at the end of April, a seven-day cruise. I went to my doctor just prior to departing, and had yet another cortisone shot into my knee. It did relieve some of the pain, and we took off for our cruise, me without the wheelchair, but with my walker. Our rooms were connected and we both had ocean-view balconies. I just absolutely love cruises. Just unpack, and at the end of the fun-filled and relaxing cruise, repack. Before we left, I had a secret surprise for my family. A huge black limo arrived at 10:30 am, to pick up my husband and me. Then we drove to pick up my sons in that black limo. Everyone was indeed surprised. When our cruise ended, the same driver showed up with a white limo, this time. In all honestly, we would have needed two cars to drive to the pier, pay for two parking spaces, for an entire week, and the sheer joy and comfort cannot be beat. Plus, when the driver came to pick us up, he called me on my unused cell phone of a week, to tell us he brought a white limo this time, and his exact location.

So back to work for all, except me and Rene'. He had been retired since 2005. More and more doctor appointments for me. I continued to get cortisone injections. The last one I received did not help at all. I was then referred to orthopedics. More tests conducted. My real estate business slowed down immensely, both due to the slow market and my health.

Chapter 64

I was scheduled for total knee replacement in July 2009. I stayed in the hospital for four days. What a surgery! The pain was intense. The health care delivered a machine to our home, that moved my leg up and down, or was it, back and forth. I placed my whole leg on it. Rene' would apply an ice bag, and Velcro it all together. And this must, I repeat, must, stay on for seven or so hours, for days, yet.

I was well cared-for. Rene' did a magnificent job. Every two days, the therapist came by to exercise my leg. I was supposed to also exercise on the days she didn't show up. Did I? "No". Also, another person came by every few days, to take my blood. Later that evening, I would receive a call from the lab, relating the amount of blood thinner pill to take until my blood was drawn again. It was a long recovery. I needed a walker for months. Eventually I progressed to a cane, which I use to this day. It is not quite a year since my knee surgery, and I still have difficulty climbing in and out of the car, getting up from chairs, or the couch. Not to mention the eight-inch scar that I acquired.

I know that within months or just a matter of a couple years, I will be confined to a wheelchair. When I rise in the morning, my back hurts so. During the night, my hips and legs hurt constantly. My husband, bless his heart, massages both legs and feet nearly every night. He knows and sees my pain.

Chapter 65

Right after Christmas of 2009, I noticed Rene' being overly tired, and absolutely no energy. After doing a little yard work, he would come inside all breathless. Sometime after the first of the year, he went up on the roof, to remove the Christmas lights. When he came inside, he again was breathless. Even taking a shower proved quite a task. He seemed withdrawn to me. I remember, teasing him "What, you didn't like your Christmas presents?"

It is just the 6th of January, and Rene' and I visit my mom. Rene' wheels her around the home. I stay behind in her room. Mom looks wonderful and knows who we are. Rene' drove on the way home. He kept wiping his sweaty hands on his jeans. We were near home, when I noticed his face was also sweaty and red. As we took the exit, he started clutching his chest. I told him to pull over or just stop in the middle of the road, at that point, I didn't care which. We switched positions and I drove him straight to our health clinic. He had a heart attack, and 911 personnel were called to transport him to the hospital. I waited until he was placed in the ambulance.

Earlier when we left our house to visit my mom, I was not wearing my blue tooth (a devise one can wear on their ear, after programming it to a cell phone). I figured I did not need it, since I was not going to drive. So, the ambulance takes off, and one of the attendants actually tells me not to follow him, because they will be going through red lights. I mean, really here –duh??? Okay, here I am some distance behind the ambulance but still within sight. I grab my cell phone to notify our sons. And, obviously I am not wearing the blue tooth. So, guess what? A motorcycle cop pulls me over.

This is a very serious offense. Especially those who text message while driving. So he asks me "why are you on the phone?" I say "You see that ambulance just turning the corner, my husband is in it. He is having a heart attack". The officer proceeds to ignore my emergency crisis. He starts to instruct me on pulling over before using a cell phone.

In the meantime, I repeat that my husband is having a heart attack and I naturally wanted to notify our sons. I did tell him I normally used a blue tooth. But due to the emergency circumstances, I did not think to hook it up, and place it in my ear, after waiting for the red light to transfer its connection. This officer is a real pill! He next asks me for my driver's license and proof of insurance. I present them, all the while nicely complaining that I needed to be with my heart-attack husband. He hands them back to me, and lastly educates me, once again, on no cell use while driving.

I arrive at emergency and wait for hours. Chris left work to join me. Matt showed up a little later. In the meantime, the only thing I knew was that Rene' suffered a heart attack. At age 60. "What was going on?" Finally around 5 pm, the doctor comes out to tell us he had three clogged arteries. They put in two stints (a balloon which is inserted near the groin area. Once inside, it inflates and deposits a stint on the heart artery, thus eliminating all blood from clotting). He would remain in intensive care through Friday, when a third stint would be inserted. On Saturday, he was released from the hospital. I really needed to change his diet. No more fast-food, nothing that came from a can or a box. Well, that is almost impossible. First off, I am still not feeling well-enough to cook meals from scratch. I also needed to eliminate sweets. The doctor also said he was diabetic. Now, lookie here, Rene' was used to a bowl of ice cream nightly. And not just two scoops either. A good large four scoops, including a banana, nut topping, cherries, chocolate syrup, and strawberry syrup. The works!

Chapter 66

About two weeks after he was home and we were successfully eating more healthy, he was complaining of a foot problem. His right foot was all red and swollen. There was a puss-filled area between his toes. When he could hardly walk on it, off we went to a podiatrist. They cleaned the area between his toes, gauzed it up proper, and gave him a walking boot to wear. We had an appointment later that same week. When they removed the gauze, it was all puffy and looked like a sac hanging there, on top of his foot. Once again, the doctor drained it. Bandaged it up and we followed up with another two appointments. Eventually, we went to a prosthesis center, where his foot was placed in mold-like clay, and a master made. That included his choice of a pair of diabetic shoes. All paid for by our health care. The shoes are quite modern and attractive. The inserts are to prevent further irritation between the toes.

To this day, we are still dealing with his heart, his diabetes, and his foot. He must monitor his diabetes daily. He takes a reading of his blood count daily. Pricks his finger and draws some blood. Then he places the tip of blood on a reading meter.

Christopher and Matthew continue to work long hours, still live together, and have no serious girlfriends. They continue to get their hair cut every month. They both dress neat and tidy. And have no tattoos or pierced body parts that I am aware of. I am very proud of my babies. Perhaps I will never see grandbabies. Only God knows. Just the other day, when I visited my mom, she asked me: "When am I going to die?" I gave her the same answer that I give myself: "Only God knows". Bless her heart, at six months from turning 93 years old, she still crochets, beautifully, too. She was getting low on some white tread, and was wondering if I should buy her some more. I, guess, thinking it would be unnecessary to purchase more, if she was going to die soon.

Chapter 67

Lastly, back to me. In March of this year (2010), I required toe bunion and hammer toe surgery. When I look back, this surgery did not even begin to compare with my other eight or nine surgeries. Let me describe my right foot. The bone where the big toe is, was extending out so much, looked like a 6th toe. The 2nd toe was bent and forming itself on top of the big toe. Arthritic condition. Yes, this was very painful. Got to where I could only wear one pair of shoes. During surgery, the doctor sawed off that extra bone protrusion, plus actually broke my 2nd toe, and stuck a three-inch post inside the toe.

I left the hospital wearing a foot boot just like my husband. When I returned for after-care examination, the doctor removed the post and asked if we wanted it. My husband said "yes". So in my jewelry case, sits this 3-inch post. It did come out clean, after all is said and done.

Chapter 68

As I sit here at age 63, I wonder and reflect on my three varied lives. Four-eyes (when I was a youngster), Anna-Banana (when I was a teenager plus young lady), or wife and mommy! Was #1 the best years of my life when I was an innocent youngster living on a farm? How about #2, when I was in my 20's and so very carefree and reckless? Or #3, wife and motherhood? Ya'all decide. I know which is my choice. As Louis Armstrong's song goes, "What a won – der – ful world. Ohhhhhhh y – e – a – h!

You may reach me at my e-mail loera4@aol.com. Please title your message Onya so that I can differentiate my mail.